Nobody Told Me
I'd Have to Sell

Nobody Told Me I'd Have to Sell

How to Sell Your
Services and Skills,
Even If
You're Not in Sales

Dick Kendall

A Birch Lane Press Book
Published by Carol Publishing Group

A Birch Lane Press Book
Published by Carol Publishing Group
Birch Lane Press is a registered trademark of Carol Communications, Inc.
Editorial Offices: 600 Madison Avenue, New York, NY 10022
Sales and Distribution Offices: 120 Enterprise Avenue, Secaucus, NJ 07094
In Canada: Canadian Manda Group, One Atlantic Avenue, Suite 105, Toronto, Ontario M6K 3E7
Queries regarding rights and permissions should be addressed to Carol Publishing Group, 600 Madison Avenue, New York, NY 10022

Carol Publishing Group books are available at special discounts for bulk purchases, sales promotion, fund-raising, or educational purposes. Special editions can be created to specifications. For details, contact: Special Sales Department, Carol Publishing Group, 120 Enterprise Avenue, Secaucus, NJ 07094

Manufactured in the United States of America

10 9 8 7 6 5 4 3 2 1

Library of Congress Cataloging-in-Publication Data

Kendall, Dick.
  Nobody told me I'd have to sell : how to sell your services and skills, even if you're not in sales / Dick Kendall.
      p. cm.
"A Birch Lane Press book."
ISBN 1-55972-302-5 (hc)
1. Selling. 2. customer relations. I. Title.
HF5438.25.K47 1995
658.85—dc20   95-19232
                                                          CIP

To my wife Jean.
Without her loving support I would never have had
the courage or the time to write this book.

Contents

Preface

"OF making many books there is no end; and much study is a weariness of the flesh": So stated the Book of Ecclesiastes. So why should I be presumptuous enough to write yet another book, particularly on selling? There are hundreds, maybe thousands, of books on the subject.

Here's why. I have always thought of selling as being bad, beneath me, if you will. So, out of college I went into chamber of commerce management, then banking, then started my own consulting business. Those were certainly not selling professions. And yet in the chambers, the banks, and certainly my own business I found what J.C. Penney is reported to have said: "Nothing happens until somebody sells something." I have had to sell most of my life.

As a bank marketing officer I found that there were a lot of people in the banking profession just like me. They didn't like the idea of selling. Yet as banking was deregulated and more competition set in, banking could only survive if someone sold something. I had to teach bankers to sell. After I started a marketing consulting firm I found that there were a lot of people who hated selling but had to sell. Architects, CPAs, engineers, business owners, and many others were in the same boat. I found, too, that if I could teach bankers to sell I could teach anybody how to sell.

The need was there for sales training for people just like me who had started out in life to be anything but a salesman. And so, over the years, I have taught literally thousands of people that selling is not only necessary but can even be an acceptable part of their lives. It is usually not selling that is the problem but their perception of what selling is all about.

And so the idea for the book was born. I did research. There were hundreds of books on selling. There were even books on selling for "non–sales executives." But there were no books on selling that understood you and me, the people who don't like the idea of selling. Those persons, who, for whatever reason, find that selling has to be included in their lives or they have no work. Or the company they work for has no business. Yet the idea of having to sell is frightening or, at least, repugnant to them.

So if you fit that mold—you don't like the idea of selling yet you have to—you have picked up the right book. I still have those feelings about selling. I still have to sell. If this describes you, too, then I understand you. I empathize with you. My experience, though, tells me that there is hope. I think you will find in these pages the answer to a problem you have to live with. If you are like many of the others I have worked with over the decades, you may even find that what I present here is not only tolerable but perhaps even fun.

Not only is the way I approach sales training different, it may be that the world in which you and I work is becoming different from what it was only a few years ago. It seems to me that the commercial world is changing. As I look at that statement it seems entirely too obvious. But change is only significant as it affects me. You might say the same thing. You might ask, "How is it changing and how does it affect me?"

Former president George Bush said that he saw a vision of a "kinder and gentler" nation. He quoted that again, by the way, at the inaugural activities as his son George W. became governor of Texas. I, too, see that vision in the world of business. There are many observers of the business world who would say that I have rather wild and unrealistic visions. There are others who agree with those visions.

Stephen Covey, in his bestselling book *The Seven Habits of Highly Effective People*, tells of his study of two hundred years of writings about success. He states, "I began to feel more and more that much of the success literature of the past fifty years was superficial.... In stark contrast, almost all the literature in the first 150 years or so focused on what could be called the Character Ethic.... The Character Ethic taught that there are basic principles of effective living, and that people can only experience true success and enduring happiness as they learn and integrate these principles into their basic character."

Covey goes on to explain the seven habits that he believes build character. "Sow a habit, you reap a character," as the Samuel Smiles quote goes. The book is excellent. My interest is not so much in that Dr. Covey wrote the book, however. There are always wise and learned men who see the way things ought to be. My interest is in its popularity. It has been number one on the *New York Times* Best Seller list.

A few years back another bestseller, *Swim With the Sharks Without Being Eaten Alive,* was written by Harvey Mackay. The book is excellent, with many wonderful ideas for conducting business better. However, what interests me is that so many people bought that title. I must assume that most of them did not consider themselves to be sharks.

One of Covey's seven habits is Think Win/Win. I first heard that expression in the book *I'm OK, You're OK,* by Thomas A. Harris, M.D. That was a pop psychology book published in 1969. The "world view" of "I'm OK, you're not OK" was Win/Lose; "I'm not OK, you're OK" was Lose/Win; and "I'm OK, you're OK" was Win/Win. It takes awhile for these ideas to filter down.

To my way of thinking, the popularity of these books and ideas is an indication that the business world is changing. The old competition in business is coming under question and being replaced by a more cooperative approach. We all are in it to win, and my winning requires my helping you win.

These ideas are reflected in the changing world trade situation. No longer is America the only producer. Other nations are increasing their productivity at a faster rate than America. There is truly a world market. This new world order will require cooperation, particularly within the borders of the United States. It will also require cooperation among nations.

This new world need for cooperation will require a new way of selling our goods and services, both here and abroad. The selling concepts included in this book are certainly not new. However, there may be a new emphasis on the relationship-building aspect of selling. That is what this book is all about. We all must sell our products and services, to be sure, but also our ideas. In the past many of us have considered the Win/Lose approach to selling. Do unto others before they can do unto you. I was never comfortable with that approach myself. Perhaps you were not, either. Now the truth is that that approach just doesn't work anymore. And so a new order comes to the business world. It is my strong desire that this book play at least a small part in this peaceful revolution.

Kahlil Gibran, who died in 1931, in his book *The Prophet,* had this to say about selling:

> And a merchant said, "Speak to us of Buying and Selling."
> And he answered and said: "...It is in exchanging the gifts of the earth that you shall find abundance and be satisfied.
> "Yet unless the exchange be in love and kindly justice, it will but lead some to greed and others to hunger."

This concept, whether it be new or not, is also part of the changing role that women are playing in the business world. Our nation has recognized the valuable contribution women can make in business. In this book I have used the terms *he* and *him* instead of the more cumbersome *he/she* and *him/her. He* and *him* are the English language's closest equivalent to neutral in discussing gender. Of course, many of my examples involve women. In those cases I have used *she* and *her.*

While it is true that probably the vast majority of business owners and CEO's that I have called on over the years have been male, this is changing. Twenty years ago, when I first started consulting with banks, the majority of my students in sales classes were male. This has already changed. Now it is closer to fifty-fifty. I think we will continue to see this change in the gender makeup of senior management and owners.

Barbara Bush, wife of the president, made these remarks at the Wellesley College Commencement in June 1990: "Somewhere out in this audience may even be someone who will one day follow in my footsteps and preside over the White House as the president's spouse. I wish him well!" I believe we may well see that in the next decade or two.

Part of the reason for all of this is the changing world order. In our society young women are brought up with better skills of cooperation than men. Young men are taught competition. In my opinion, this competitive spirit, though good in some cases, is losing its importance in the business world. Cooperation and relationship-building skills will be more necessary in the future. Women bring a natural set of skills to this new marketplace. Many of us men were never comfortable with the competitive role anyway. For those who feel that way, this book is for you. If you are female, I think you will find the concepts presented here to be helpful, comfortable, and encouraging. If you are male, you may find a new comfort in the selling you have to do.

The ideas about selling presented here are not new to me. There has been selling going on since Eve persuaded Adam to eat the forbidden fruit. (Of course, she may have used a premium for added enticement.) I am indebted to the many teachers and mentors I have had over the years. I have given some specific credit where possible. I wish I could give credit to all. If I have made a contribution here it is that I have approached the subject from the standpoint of those of us who think that selling is bad. I understand that frame of mind. I have had to deal with it in my own life. I hope my viewpoint will be of value to you.

Acknowledgments

THIS book is the result of many years of both selling and teaching others to sell. I have learned so much from so many over the years that I hesitate to name any names because I will have to leave out most of them.

Bosses and partners I have worked with come to mind. I particularly think of Don German, a man who knows much about both selling and training and who has willingly shared that knowledge with me. Many of the ideas in this book came directly from Don.

Lee Estis, a former partner and management trainer who always sells himself to his clients, his students, and to me. Lee has always been available to help with any new challenge.

Laird Landon, another former partner, so often has encouraged me to believe in myself and what I do. He helped me put together the first really professional version of my sales training seminar and continues to be a helper and friend.

A number of bosses believed in me and gave me opportunities: Gerald Smith, Jay Crager, Willie Whitehead, and Russell Willis.

John Floyd and the people at John M. Floyd and Associates have helped me take my training and marketing skills to new levels of effectiveness and have put up with my writing when they needed my time.

I especially want to thank my parents, Bill and Lois Kendall, who instilled in me the basic values on which this book is based, love for others and giving at least as much as you get. Thanks to my daughters, Peggy Kendall and Susan Morrow, who have taught me much of what I know about selling and have encouraged me in the writing of this book.

I wish I had space to name all the students and clients I have served over the years whose hard work has produced the successes that helped keep me going. I have learned much from them all. People like Bill Dean, Jimmy Blanchard, Bob Chaney, Nancy Buntin, Lon Knowles, and Rick Riseden come to mind but are only a few of thousands. Thanks to you all.

Kevin McDonough, my editor at Carol Publishing, and the other editors have spent many hours improving this book. Kevin believed in me and the book. I needed that.

Nobody Told Me
I'd Have to Sell

1

I Couldn't Get a Real Job

NOBODY buys anything from us unless they have a problem they think we can solve. If you like to help people solve problems, read on.

I am a seminar leader. In my seminars I get to know people and learn why they came to the seminar. I can't do that here. I don't know why you are reading this book. I'll have to make some assumptions:

1. You're a professional (banker, architect, engineer, CPA, lawyer, entrepreneur, etc.).
2. You don't like to sell and never wanted to be a salesman. That was one reason for getting your degree.
3. You have to sell. The boss says so. The growth of your company requires it. The sales department wants you to, etc.
4. You have a slight hope that this book will teach you something about selling that will make it less painful or frightening.
5. Most of the above four assumptions are right, but the real reason is that your boss handed you the book and said, "Read it!"

If these assumptions fit you, then you have come to the right source. You and I will have fun together. We're a lot alike.

If, on the other hand, you like selling and are looking for some new gimmick or technique that will help you close another deal, manipulate another unsuspecting prospect, or pack your coffers with more of someone else's gold, then take this book back and get a refund. It's not for you.

Let me share a little of my selling experience. My parents raised me to hate selling, salesmen, and the whole selling game. In spite

3

of that I have been selling something since I was a sophomore in college. (That is, if you don't count my selling *Houston Press* subscriptions in the fourth grade so I could win a pocketknife. I didn't get the knife, but I did win a set of ruby glasses and a pitcher that I gave to my mom. She gave it back years later. The set is now a valuable collector's item. This has little to do with the purpose of the book, but I thought you might find it interesting.)

The summer after my freshman year in college I spent days pounding the pavement looking for work. I had to have work or I couldn't go back to school the next fall. One day I came home and told my mother I had taken a job selling Child Craft Books.

"You did what?" I thought she was going to faint. She sat down. Her face was full of anguish. It was the same look she had when I was seven and my brother and I had a big fight at the church Christmas pageant.

"But, Mom, I couldn't find a *real* job." I really believed that. Selling wasn't a real job. It was something closely akin to bank robbery. But I had to have a job.

That was the most miserable summer of my life. Now don't get me wrong. It was not the books I disliked. I had grown up with Child Craft Books. I loved them. I believed in them. I thought only underprivileged children did not have them. So why was I so miserable selling them?

Part of the reason was the training I received. I'll never forget it. I had been recruited by what I thought then was an old woman. She was probably all of fifty, but what do kids know. I'm sure she had been successful in selling Child Craft. She might even have been successful in training some people to sell them. But she did not understand me. Here's what happened.

We spent all of one day in the training. She spent most of the morning teaching me about the books.

In case you don't know, Child Craft Books are a multivolume set that includes everything from child psychology to how to entertain kids on a rainy day. One of my earliest and fondest recollections as a child was sitting on my mother's lap while she read poetry from the Child Craft book of children's poems. The beautiful illustrations are still in my memory. Volumes on Whether to call the doctor and what to do till he gets there, early reading, crafts, creativity, etc., make the set essential for parents of young children.

So half a day spent meandering through my memories and expanding my knowledge of a good product was fairly pleasant. Then we started the training on sales "techniques." The very word made me feel that I was going to learn to do something to someone—something that they would not like or thank me for. I was right.

We spent the rest of the day learning every technique for manipulating, frightening, cajoling, and tricking young mothers into signing a contract and a check. (In those days, most mothers stayed at home and the fathers went to work. So the typical victim, uh, prospect, was a young mother.) The training went against every value I had developed since early childhood. But I had to have the job, so I listened.

Then she finished the training with her best coach's pep talk. "Dick, you are going into battle. I've taught you how to win. I want you to think of that young mother's living room as a battlefield. If you use all the weapons I've given you today and use them skillfully, that young mother is going to be scared not to buy. She'll write a check and you will be the winner.

"But if you don't remember what you learned here today, if you think you've got a better way, then that mother won't write a check. You'll leave empty-handed. She will win and you will lose." I almost threw up. But I had to have the job, so I listened.

I may be writing this book today because of that woman. Not because she taught me anything about selling. But because she taught how not to teach others how to sell.

If only she had said to me, "Dick, we have the finest set of books a young family could ever hope to own. You don't have children yet, but let me tell you about bringing that baby home from the hospital. It is marvelous and exciting, but it is frightening, too.

"You have such wonderful hope for that child. He or she is going to be president of the United States, a great philosopher, teacher, or perhaps the pope. You want that child to have every advantage, to be ahead of the others in school, to excel, to develop every talent and skill.

"But you're afraid, too, Dick. There are so many diseases, accidents, learning problems, and conflicts. How will you handle every situation to steer that young child in the right direction? You know, Dick, kids are the most intricate mechanisms in the world—

and there's no instruction booklet. Believe me, you look for one. As intricate and delicate as they are, kids are made with unskilled labor.

"Now, Dick, here is where your selling skills come in. If you can go into that living room with an understanding of where that young mother is coming from, of her fears and her aspirations for that child or those children; if you can ask her questions to learn more about her specific concerns; get her talking about them and listen, really listen; then, if you can give her feedback to show that you've heard her, she probably will be willing to listen to you tell her about the wonderful set of books that have helped millions of mothers in similar situations.

"Then if you carefully match your knowledge of these books with your new knowledge of her problems and show her how these books will solve those problems for her, then she'll write you a check, sign the contract, and bless you every time she opens them. You will win and so will she."

I call the selling technique I have just outlined the Win/Win approach as opposed to the Win/Lose approach that the woman actually taught me. I could live with the Win/Win approach. If I had known it then, I probably would have had a better summer. But more about that later.

At Baylor University I majored in philosophy. I was a ministerial student but never realized that career. I know now that I chose that career initially because I wanted to help people solve problems. I still do.

Baylor has a good business school. I remember, though, thinking that people who majored in marketing were a little strange; maybe not quite human, certainly not as "human" as philosophy majors.

One of the few jobs my philosophy degree qualified me for in 1957 was that of chamber of commerce manager. I went to work on the staff of a chamber in San Angelo, Texas. Later I was manager of chambers of commerce in three other small Texas towns. I didn't know until years later that a chamber manager's primary work is selling—selling businessmen on joining, selling committee members on working, selling the city to new industry.

It was a good thing I didn't know that. I might have hated the job.

I didn't hate the job. I loved it. It was a good thing my mother didn't know I was selling. She was very proud of me.

Then a bank in town asked me to be vice president of marketing. I still didn't want to sell anything, but being vice president of a bank seemed okay. My mother was still proud.

Shortly after I went to work for the bank, a group of Houston businessmen bought control of it. They put in a new president and made many changes. We doubled the size of the bank and took the market away from the competition. Since I was vice president of marketing I took credit for the success.

The group asked me to move to Houston and set up marketing programs for the other banks controlled by the group. Later I helped that group put a bank holding company together called Allied Bancshares.

In 1984 *Fortune* magazine named Allied the eleventh-most-successful service company for the previous decade. My marketing programs, selling, and sales training helped make that happen. But I'm getting ahead of myself.

At that first bank-marketing job in the small town of Conroe, Texas, I learned something. I had to sell. More important, I learned that everyone in that bank had to sell. And I had to teach them how. What those people taught me in turn is the basis of this book.

Those bankers thought they did not want to be salesmen. I thought I didn't want to be a salesman. We were all wrong.

What we didn't want was to be manipulative, tricky, to make people do what they didn't want to do. What we did want was to help people solve problems by building good relationships with them. We didn't know that this is what real selling is all about. I know that now. I hope that you will agree with me by the time you finish this book.

Chances are you have built good relationships with people by helping them solve problems. You combine your knowledge and experience with your clients' or peers' knowledge of their problem to find solutions. In the process you build good relationships. That process is selling in its highest form. You already know how. The next chapter should prove that to you.

2

A Good Client Is Hard to Find

DURING my days at Allied Bancshares there was the case of Wilford the loan officer. (The name has been changed to protect the innocent. If your name is Wilford I'm sorry. Not for the affront. I'm just sorry your name is Wilford). Will (we'll call him that for short) was an outstanding loan officer. He could answer any question asked about any of his customers. He had been to their offices. He had seen their operations. He had asked questions and understood their businesses. He was a good loan officer and he knew it. Will would not make a sales call.

In those days we were still a small, upstart banking company going head-to-head with the bigger banks. Calling on their customers was a necessity if we were to grow. We called on the relatively small to medium-sized businesses that the larger banks were not servicing well.

"I'm not a salesman. I can't sell," Will would counter when I would ask him to make a call. "Why don't you hire some hotshot sales type to make the calls?"

I talked to Will's customers. I asked them what they thought about Will. "He's fantastic!" they would answer. "He's the best loan officer I've ever had. He knows my business as well as I do. I feel like he's almost a partner."

"How do you think Will would do as a salesman?" I asked.

"Huh? I just told you. He's fantastic. He's the best salesman I've ever seen. I wish I could afford to hire him."

You see, the problem wasn't Will's inability to sell. The problem was Will's concept of what selling is all about. Now let's look at your concept of selling. Would you agree that the end result of good selling is a loyal customer? In other words, if I go out and make sales calls and am successful, would you agree that my measure of that success would be a customer loyal to my company? I mean a customer that I could count on to come to my business whenever he or she had a problem that I could solve.

I know you have some loyal customers in your business. These may be individuals or other companies for which you provide a product or service, or they may be internal customers, another department, a boss, a peer, the board of directors. But just to make sure we have the concept down I'll go into it in a little more detail. A few examples might better make the point.

Example A

Here is one I found while working out a marketing plan for one of my clients. When I write a marketing plan I call and talk to my client's customers. Among other questions I always ask, "If you had the same situation over again, who would you call next time?" If the customer quickly names my client I know I have a loyal customer. This particular client leases office trailers and temporary offices to the construction trade, petrochemical plants, hospitals, and anyone else who has need for space on a temporary basis. The trailers are hauled out to the customer's site and set up similar to a mobile home.

A couple of years ago a major petrochemical plant had an explosion. People were killed. The damage was in the millions. The publicity was nationwide. This company had been a customer of my client but only casually. They were far from exclusive. The next day the facilities manager at the plant called my client. He was distraught. He had been up all night. The president of the company had called twice. Reporters and TV cameras were outside his office. He needed temporary office space right away. He didn't have time for negotiation, credit checks, red tape, permits, and so on.

This was his third call to an office-space supplier. It was now late in the afternoon the day after the explosion. But my client's branch manager had done his homework. He had been to the plant on several occasions. He knew the players.

In my marketing study I had interviewed this branch manager.

He liked a hands-on approach. If someone called asking for office space and seemed hesitant, he would ask to see a sketch, maybe on a napkin. If the caller said yes, he would ask to come see it. His real need was to see the person, see the company. He felt it was easier to understand problems if he could see them.

He had done this with this plant facilities manager. None of his competitors had. Now the extra effort was about to pay off.

My client was ready. They not only had the offices, they circumvented all of the red tape, called in personnel who had already gone home for the evening, and delivered the office trailers by 2:00 A.M. the next day. When I called the facilities manager and asked who he would call the next time he needed office space, what do you think he said? My client, of course. That's a loyal customer. Perhaps you didn't think that meeting the needs of clients this way—visiting the plant, knowing the players, understanding the operations—is selling. But remember, we said that the end result of good selling is a loyal customer. In this story we ended up with a loyal customer. There must have been some selling going on. But I'm sneaking up on you. Let's look at another example of a loyal customer.

Example B

This story is about one of my loyal customers. He didn't start out that way, believe me. It's about a banker in a small town in the South. Coincidentally, the town is about the same distance from a major metropolitan area as Conroe is from Houston. There were other similarities to the situation I had found with the bank in Conroe several years before. For one thing the bank was the second bank in a very competitive situation, and like the one in Conroe, it was a poor second. The big bank was growing faster and was seen by the community as the only leader. When the bank was started back in the thirties, three of the directors were named Ketchem, Holdem, and Cheatham. That is true. The townsfolk have made much of it over the years. However, you don't hear that quoted near as much now as you did when I first arrived. The bankers knew they had problems. It was obvious to them at the end of every year when the bank reports were printed in the local paper. They were losing ground and losing it fast. They called me in to do some training of their lobby personnel (easy folks to blame) and perhaps propose some solutions. I suggested that I'do a marketing study and help them write a marketing plan.

In a marketing study I usually start with confidential interviews of a percentage of the personnel at all levels of management and line employees. In this case I remember interviewing about seventeen of the sixty-odd officers and employees. After the first few interviews I thought I had an idea of the problem. After seventeen I knew I did. It seemed that the only feedback personnel got from the president was to be chewed out in the weekly meeting if they did something wrong. Consequently, everybody in the bank had learned exactly how much they had to do to keep from being fired, and that was all they would produce. If they went beyond that they would get their heads chopped off...in public. I asked the president if we could have lunch. On the way to the restaurant we exchanged pleasantries about the community. At the same time my mind was running through the possibilities. I could have lied. But as we develop our ideas about what makes up a loyal customer relationship, the word *trust* nearly always comes up. Trust is not based on lies. So after we ordered lunch it was obvious he wanted to know what I had learned.

"Lon," (that is his real name, by the way) I said, "you asked me to find out what's wrong with your bank. I'm not sure how to put this...but *you* are what's wrong with your bank."

In the years that have passed since that lunch I have heard Lon tell this story, too. In his version he says that he didn't know whether to invite me into the alley for a fight or not, but he was sure he would never pay my fee.

He did pay my fee. To his credit he owned up to his management problems. He changed. He allowed me to tell the whole story when making my report to the staff. He coined the phrase "negative motivation." Whenever the old management style would crop up, you would hear "negative motivation" whispered in the background, and the manager would back off. As you might guess, Lon's management style had rubbed off on middle management. The changes Lon made had to be passed down as well.

Together we wrote a marketing plan that management followed religiously. I did some sales and customer-service training as well as management training. I trained the marketing director in her job, and she was excellent. The results were spectacular. When I first met Lon the bank was worth about $40 million in total assets with an annual profit of about $150,000. Since then, the bank has tripled in size, taken the leadership position in the community, and in a recent year made a profit of close to $2 million. When Lon thinks of marketing and training, he calls me. I have told him that the farther I get from his community the more credit I take for his success. The truth is it took both of us working together to solve the problems. Lon is my loyal customer. At this point you may be asking, "What does this have to do with selling?" My answer is, "Everything." Remember we said that a loyal customer is the end result of good selling.

"Yes," you say, "but what does it have to do with my making sales calls?"

My answer, again, is, "Everything." A good sales call leads to the discovery of a client's problem, your solution, and a sale.

Example C

A friend of mine bought a beautiful lot. That is, part of it was beautiful. It fronted on a busy street that was near a lower-income neighborhood. The back of the lot, however, overlooked a beautiful canyon that seemed far removed from the world. The lot had problems other than the busy street. It sloped too rapidly into the canyon.

My friend had already begun to look for ways to fill the back part of the lot to form a level pad for the home he wanted to build. But before he did that he decided to hire an architect to design the home.

The architect looked at the lot. He listened to my friend and his wife discuss their dreams about their home. While listening to the dreams he learned that the couple were both busy with careers and were both involved in the community. They had bought the lot primarily for the serenity offered by the canyon. They pictured themselves spending their rare free Saturday mornings having coffee on a patio overlooking the canyon listening to the mourning doves, watching the ground squirrels and armadillos, and maybe even spotting a fox.

After some study the architect found that he could excavate the front of the lot instead of filling the back. This actually placed the entire house almost totally below street level. Then, by designing an

S-curve drive so cars could negotiate the rather steep entrance and by planting large cedar plants along the drive, the house was all but hidden from the street. As he suspected, the noise from the busy street was absorbed by the plantings and went over the top of the house. This gave the couple a quiet, privacy, and serenity that was even greater than they had hoped for.

To this day my friends enjoy their serene Saturday mornings, and the architect's name is spoken almost in reverence to every visitor with whom they share their canyon. In the finest sense of the word these people are loyal customers (architects use the term *client*) for the architect.

Now if you happen to be an architect you are probably saying, "Of course. This is what architects are for. I've solved many problems like this. But what does it have to do with selling? I don't understand." In answer to that I remind you that we started off chapter 1 by saying that people will buy nothing from us unless they have a problem they think we can solve. The trick is to bring this problem-solving approach into the sales call.

Now that you have seen some examples of loyal customers, think of one of your own. I use the term *customers* here in its broadest sense. If you are an architect, lawyer, or engineer you may call them clients. If you're a doctor you call them patients. It doesn't matter what you call them. They are all people who have problems for which you have a solution.

Or you may not deal directly with customers at all. The customer for you could be another department in your company, a boss, your peers. Anybody that you have to sell solutions to will do.

In this context think of customers that you would term loyal. Customers who will always come back to you when they have the kind of problem or need for which they came to you the first time. Do you have one, or several, in mind? Good. Now name them. Picture them in detail. Remember your work with them in the past. Pretend that they are in the room with you.

Now I want you to do a simple little exercise. Write down in the margin of this book all the reasons that you know these people are loyal to you. Why will they come back or at least recommend you to their friends who have similar problems or needs? In other words, what are the elements of a loyal customer? Go ahead. Take a minute to write them down. I'll wait.

Got your list? Good. I have used this exercise for groups all over the country in all kinds of businesses with all levels and kinds of education and in all kinds of disciplines. Basically the lists tend to be about the same. I'll give you the list of words I've collected over the years and you see if your words fit. I bet they do:

We solved their problem: (Some people say "We met their needs." That's OK for now.) This one seems basic and it is. People only buy from us because they have problems they think we can solve. It doesn't matter whether you help a president change his management style or you are an exterminator and get rid of someone's bugs.

We maintained high quality: It's not just that we solved their problems. It's that we did it well. We lived up to their expectations or exceeded them. If there was a problem with our product or service we made it good. With all of the talk about quality these days you would think it was something the Japanese invented. It's not. Many of my clients could have written the book on quality and live it every day of their lives.

Our price is right: Now this one deserves even more discussion. Does this mean we're the cheapest? Probably not. Granted, we won't get away with gouging our customers just because they're loyal. But the "right price" often means something other than the cheapest. Think about your own purchases. Do you always buy the cheapest? Probably not.

There is a marvelous story about a hardware store in Conroe called Everett's Hardware. It is what is left of Everett's Mercantile from the turn of the century (the twentieth, not the twenty-first). In the early days you could buy everything from groceries to horse collars at Everett's Mercantile. When I moved to Conroe in 1962, you could still buy horse collars at Everett's. Maybe you still can.

Everett's was the kind of place you just had to go to on Saturday. I remember seeing a friend there on Saturday morning and then again on Saturday afternoon. When he saw me the second time he said, "It's just not a Saturday without at least two trips to Everett's." We both laughed.

I went into Everett's one Saturday with the valve assembly from my commode. I told the man in the plumbing department I needed a replacement. He said, "OK. We've got that, but tell me what your problem is." After I explained how the commode was behaving he took a look at the valve assembly. He unscrewed a piece and took out a washer.

"If you want a new assembly I'll be happy to sell you one. But based on what you told me and the looks of this washer all you need is a new washer." I bought the washer for fifteen cents. I probably could have bought one at a discount store for ten or eleven cents. The assembly might have been a few dollars cheaper at a discount store, too. Now, Conroe didn't have a discount store at the time. But if there had been a discount store handy I probably would have gone to Everett's anyway. What I wanted was to have my problem solved. I don't know about you, but when I'm spending my Saturday with my arms in a commode tank, saving a few dollars is not high on my priority list.

Buddy Mark Everett was one of the surviving heirs who ran the store. (In East Texas many men have two names and one of them usually starts with "B.") In the late sixties, when Houston was expanding toward Conroe, the freeway was completed, and shopping centers were taking customers from the old downtown square, Buddy Mark came to my office. I don't think he wanted my advice. He just needed to talk.

"If I stay in business I'm going to have to expand, remodel, and add parking," he said. "The way this town is growing it's just a matter of time before one of those discount chain stores comes in, and I just can't compete with their prices. I'm afraid I'll be run out of business then and any investment I make now will be down the tubes."

I could tell he had given the matter a lot of thought and was really concerned. He didn't ask for my advice but I gave him some anyway. "Buddy," I said, "you spend the money and be sure you have plenty of parking. You run a good store. People need what you have. They trust you. You have trained your employees to be really helpful. Price isn't the only thing people come to a hardware store for."

I don't know whether I had any influence, but Buddy Mark remodeled and expanded. Not long after that a discount chain store did come to town. I don't live in Conroe anymore but I drove through there a few years back. The discount store is boarded up. You still can't find a place to park at Everett's on Saturdays.

By the way, there is a hardware store in Houston called Bering's

Hardware. They have the same philosophy that Everett's has. They are known for high quality and equally high prices. During the lowest point in the Houston economy in the mid-eighties, Bering's built a second store and doubled its capacity. Both stores are booming today. So much for "the right price" and "cheapest."

We understand their needs and problems: This one often comes up in the seminars. It may well be on your list. I hope so. If we are going to solve our customer's problems we have to know what they are and understand them. Beyond that we have to know our customers, what they want, how they feel.

We care about our customers: This may not be on your list, but you'll probably add it now. If we take the time and make the effort to understand our customers they will assume that we care about them. We have to care or we won't be patient enough to listen and understand them. One of my seminar participants said one time, "People don't care how much we know until they know how much we care." I agree.

We have become friends: This is often the case. Lon has become a good friend of mine over the years, as is true of many of my clients. I have stayed in his beach house. Anytime I'm in his state we try to get together for dinner. I like Lon personally. I'm sure he likes me. Do you play golf with your customers or invite them to your parties?

Trust: This is a big one. It works both ways, doesn't it. They trust us, but we trust them, too. In fact, we may be personally hurt if they go to a competitor. They often don't ask the price when they have a problem for us to solve. They just know we will be fair.

You may have other things on your list: We helped them start their business; we helped them get their present job; we won an award for the building we built for them, product we created, etc.; we go to all their grand openings and they go to ours; we use their services or buy their products; they recommend us to their friends—the lists can go on. But most of these additions to the list can be fitted into one of the above categories. Try it with your list.

Basically I find that most of the lists are very similar. What we find is that when we talk about a loyal customer we are talking about a synergistic relationship.

The best way I know to define the word *synergy* is with an example. I came in from the yard one time and I had one arm loaded with stuff and the other hand was dirty. I couldn't put the stuff down until I washed my dirty hand. Have you ever tried to wash one hand? It's hard to do and takes awhile. You put two hands together under the faucet and they get very clean very fast. That is a synergistic relationship. We have created something new and better because we got together.

Most of the people who come to my seminars and those of you for whom this book is written are good at building these relationships. You like building these relationships. You do it well. Much of the joy of your work comes from helping people solve problems and watching a relationship grow. You count these relationships as part of your assets, and well you should.

Now, what does all this have to do with selling? Well, remember you agreed that a loyal customer is the end result of selling? If you have loyal customers, or clients, then, who do you think sold them? You did, of course. This whole chapter has two purposes. First, to let you know that you already know how to sell. And second, to let you know that selling is no more or less than building synergistic relationships through the process of understanding problems and finding solutions to them. One hand washing the other. Sounds too easy, doesn't it?

I hope, too, that you are beginning to see that selling is helping people define their problems and working with them jointly to find a solution. This understanding and problem solving is the stuff of which relationships are made.

Remember our friend Wilford, the banker I introduced at the beginning of this chapter? He did not understand this. He thought that selling was something you do *to* people. Some people come into my seminars expecting to learn "techniques" for manipulating the sale to get what they want at another's expense. They expect "twenty-seven ways to overcome objections."

Instead I believe in helping people learn to take their problem-solving and relationship-building skills out into the selling arena.

In *Swim With the Sharks Without Being Eaten Alive,* Harvey Mackay says, "The mark of a good salesperson is that his customer doesn't regard him as a salesperson at all, but a trusted and indispensable adviser, an auxiliary employee who, fortunately, is on someone else's payroll."

So if by this time you have begun to open your mind, even a small amount, to the possibility that selling is something you can live with, we have spent this time well. If you suspected that I was going to subtly sneak into your mind the idea that it is all right to manipulate someone else for the purpose of profit, I hope you are glad to be wrong.

3

Why Do They Buy?
Why Don't They Buy?

Now let's go back to our original premise, "No one buys anything from us unless they have a problem they think we can solve." If we can understand why people choose to buy something to solve a problem, we will understand what we have to do in order to get involved in that process.

When we want to sell something to people, we actually want them to change their behavior. If they are buying from someone else (someone else is solving their problem), we want them to buy from us instead. If they are not buying anything to solve the problem, we want them to buy from us in order to solve their problem. Thus we can rephrase our original statement to read, "People will not change their behavior unless they have a problem that they think changing their behavior will solve."

Therefore, if we are to understand the buying process and how we are to get involved in it, we have to understand why people change behavior (or buy something). We call this the "cycle of behavior change." It can also be called "work" or "activity" or "life." It is what we human beings do all the time.

Basically we are talking about motivation. Why are people motivated to do what they do? It might be helpful here to discuss motivation. Not that I know everything there is to know about what motivates people. I'm as perplexed as you are. I often say things like, "I wonder what got into them?" I don't know. One thing I have come to understand is that whatever "got into them" made sense to them at the time.

Let's look at Abraham Maslow's classic work on human motivation. Maslow wanted to find out what motivated people to succeed in life. He defined that success very broadly to include far more than just material or financial success. In my opinion, Maslow's greatest contributions to the wealth of human knowledge are his theories about the hierarchy of human needs.

Maslow proposed that there are five categories of needs that all human beings have, and that the desire to meet these needs is what motivates all of us to do what we do. Maslow expressed these needs in a hierarchy because he found that people tend to meet the lower-level needs first and then move on the next level. Now, since none of these needs are ever fully met, the model is a dynamic—people's motivations are constantly moving up and down the hierarchy.

Someone else, I am told, put the hierarchy in the form of a pyramid, and here is how it looks.

WHY PEOPLE DO WHAT THEY DO

Maslow's Hierarchy of Needs

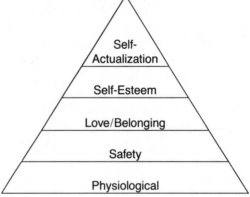

Maslow found that the lowest level of unmet needs will be the most demanding. In other words, the physiological needs, for food, water, shelter, and clothing, if not met, will demand our greatest attention. Safety needs will be next, and so on.

However, this is not a static model. If lights flashed on each of these five levels as it was providing our motivation, the lights would be in constant motion.

Maslow called the two lower needs "negative motivators." If they are not met they are strong motivators, but if they are pretty well met we tend to take them for granted. Most of your customers and associates have these two levels of need pretty well taken care of. Granted, they all have a desire to keep their businesses going or to stay employed, but these are probably not the primary motivators in why they buy your product or service.

Let's look at the upper three levels of need. Love and belonging: the need to know that our family cares about us, that the group at the office makes us feel part of the team. If that isn't enough, we join the Lions Club, the bowling team, or other organizations. The love-and-belonging need is often partly a motivator for buying goods and services. Part of the reason that I bank where I do is because the president runs out of his office and greets me with a warm handshake and a smile. The vaults and interest rates are about the same down the street.

The self-esteem need: I want to accomplish something and I want people to know I have done it. I want to drive a new Lexus so my neighbors will know I've arrived. Granted, this need is more complex than I have described but you get the idea. Certainly many of our goods and services are bought to satisfy this need.

The self-actualization need: I want to be the best Dick Kendall I can be and I don't care who knows it. I want to reach my full potential, stretch the limits, reach the heights. I remember a sailing trip I took several years ago. My two buddies and I were trying to decide whether to go out across open waters to a faraway island, my first shot at blue-water sailing, out of sight of land night and day. My buddies decided to leave the decision to me. I thought of all the ways I could die out there: storms, pirates, sharks. And then I thought, "What if I don't go and I die anyway. Or what if I don't go and I don't die. I'll have to live with the knowledge that I didn't go." I went. Now I know that if you have circumnavigated the world alone in a sailboat, that might not impress you. But it changed my life. That was a choice to self-actualize. (By the way, I never saw a pirate or a shark.)

I chartered that sailboat (bought that service) partially from a need to prove myself.

So these are the needs that motivate us to change (or buy). Without these needs—or if these needs are all pretty well filled—we aren't motivated to change (or buy) anything. Fortunately for those of us who need to sell our products or services, few people can say that all these needs are met.

One other small idea that becomes obvious when we study Maslow is that people do what they do for their own reasons—not ours. That seems so basic and simplistic that it almost seems unnecessary to mention. But I am constantly hearing someone come back from a sales call saying something like, "I can't understand why he didn't buy our deal. I gave him every reason in the book. It was obviously the 'right' choice." People do what they do for their reasons, not ours—ever.

I hear sales trainers and managers talk about finding out what the customers' needs are. I already know. Maslow has told me. What I want to know is, how do you translate those needs into goals. Because it is the reaching of certain goals you perceive that will help you meet those needs. So all of us are constantly setting goals. We may not be aware of the fact that we have these goals. Certainly many of them are subconscious. But we have them if for no other reason than to assure our Maslow pyramid that we're working on meeting our needs. But setting goals is only the first thing we do to satisfy our basic Maslow needs. I'll illustrate.

This is a rather simple illustration (perhaps too simple), but it shows how I translate one of my needs into a goal and then that goal into the definition of a problem and then get motivated to change my behavior in order to solve the problem, to reach the goal, to meet the need. Here goes:

I travel a lot in my work. I have stayed in fine hotels and motels and not-so-fine hotels and motels. Examples of each lie within forty miles of each other in South Texas. There is the Hyatt Regency on the River Walk in San Antonio, one of my favorite hotels, and there is the Marv Inn, a motel in Pleasanton, Texas, one of my least favorite. When you pull up in front of a motel and see a big sign that says AIR-CONDITIONED ROOMS, you know you're in trouble.

Anyway, the Marv Inn and the Hyatt Regency do have four things in common—the walls. And they begin to close in on you after you have been there for awhile. Now this story is about the four walls of the Hyatt Regency, a very nice hotel. The rooms are great and so is the service. But what makes it unique is its huge atrium lobby, which has a huge two-block-long fountain running through it that connects the Alamo with the river. It is beautiful.

I was in San Antonio several years ago conducting a series of training seminars for Frost Bank. It's a big bank and it took us a long time to train all of the bank's officers. I was there for several weeks. Now, when you work for a bank as a consultant, the president usually takes you out to dinner the first night. The next night an executive vice president takes you out. The third night a vice president is assigned to take you to dinner. After that you are on your own, one of the guys.

I had gotten to that point. The seminar had ended for the day. The bankers said, "See you tomorrow, Dick." I was on my own for the evening. I went back to the Hyatt. I did some work, made some phone calls, went to dinner. I came back to the room and put on my pajamas. But I wasn't quite ready to go to bed. Suddenly the thought of an ice cream cone entered my head. Maslow's pyramid was at work.

If you've ever been to the River Walk in San Antonio, you surely know about Justin's ice cream shop. The *J* in the sign looks like a map of Italy. Italian ice cream. It makes other ice cream taste like skim milk. Just reading about the butter-fat content will increase your cholesterol level. It's wonderful.

Here is what's going on. My Maslow need for love and belonging is not being met. I am lonesome. Now at the time I was not at all aware of that. I did not see a little light flashing over the "love and belonging" segment of my Maslow pyramid. I merely thought of an ice cream cone. My mind had set a goal for me. Reaching that goal, in my perception, would help meet the love and belonging need that was going unmet. I would take 'little Dicky' by the hand and bring him across the river for an ice cream cone.

My theory is that every time I find myself staring into an open refrigerator I'm experiencing this dynamic. I don't have any real proof of that theory, but it works in my life.

So this is how we translate our basic needs into life. We set goals. So when I call on you I don't have to know your needs. I want to know your goals. Where are you headed? What do you want to accomplish? Where do you see your business in the next few years?

We all have goals: business goals, personal goals, goals for our family, for our kids, goals for our personal education, goals for recreation. We have hundreds of goals. Every few years I take my own advice and write down goals for my business. But many of my goals are floating rather nebulously around the back of my brain.

They are *all* motivating me to some degree. The ones I bring to the front of my mind are motivating me the most. The ones you ask me questions about and get me talking about come to the front of my mind.

There is another factor that motivates people to change behavior (or buy). That factor is the defining of a problem that is keeping them from reaching a goal. In the illustration above I had a problem that was keeping me from reaching my goal of the ice cream cone— I was not dressed to go out.

Now I grant you that it did not take me long to define that problem. However, the recognition of the problem motivated me to change in order to reach a solution. In this case, I had to change clothes.

Let's talk about the motivation that takes place when we define a problem. We are problem-solving mechanisms as human beings. If you have trouble accepting that fact, think of how long you can watch somebody try to fix something before saying, "Let me have that screwdriver. I think I see how to do it."

Another illustration to prove the point is the actuarial tables of the insurance companies. I read several years ago that the tables showed that within eighteen months of retirement, half of all retirees are dead. Retirement often brings the end of problems that we are used to solving. Therefore, in my opinion, if we don't pick up a new set of problems after retirement our body looks around and says, "Hey, we don't have anything to do. Let's check out."

I've studied retirees some since I'm getting closer to that age. It has been my experience that successful retirees find a whole new set of problems. They may start gardening, find a new job, or get involved in volunteer work. The lucky ones find someone else's problems to solve. By the way, I think it also helps to have a good sense of humor along with the problems.

My dad is a good example of having both someone else's problems and a sense of humor. At this writing Dad is eighty-seven years old. My mother is eighty-four. Dad's been retired for nearly twenty-five years. They are so busy I have to make an appointment to see them. I called them the other day to show them some pictures of a vacation my wife and I had taken. It was three days before they could work us in.

Mother and Dad are involved in all kinds of charities. They are active in their church. They help solve all kinds of problems for people who come to the Texas Medical Center. For one thing, their church provides housing for people who are in Houston for extended cancer treatment. Dad is in charge of finding the housing. That's just one example. He's always driving people who can't drive anymore to church meetings. He told me the other day, "Dick, I get so tired of driving these *old* people around."

We are problem solvers. I meet my Maslow needs by reaching out for a particular goal. I have hundreds of goals floating around in my head, but I pick one at a time to work toward. At one time I may pick one because it will get me some needed cash to provide for my physiological needs. At another time I may pick one to meet some of the needs at a higher level.

But once I have picked a goal to work on, I run into problems that are keeping me from reaching that goal. A goal, by definition, is unmet. It is unmet because of one or more problems. The problem may simply be not having enough time to reach the goal. Or it may be far more complex.

At any rate, when I go to work I reach for a work-related goal and I begin to sort out the problems. I take one of those problems and begins to study it and define it. As I look more closely at that problem I begin to feel a motivation to find a solution to that problem. The more I study it, worry it, define it, the more motivated I am to solve it.

So now I have a double motivation. I am motivated to reach the goal because I perceive that it will meet my Maslow need. But now that I have begun to dig into the problem that is keeping me from reaching that goal, I am motivated a second time. This time just to solve the problem because solving problems is what I do.

I have hundreds of goals: business goals, personal goals, educational goals, physical goals—all kinds of goals. I have subgoals, the reaching of which will get me closer to reaching a major goal. At any given time I may start to work toward one of these goals. I choose that goal for a variety of reasons: my corresponding Maslow need is feeling unmet; someone else has superimposed a deadline on me; its just feels right; etc.

As I move toward my chosen goal, I hit a problem. I take the problem out and define it, massage it, study it. The double motivation kicks in and I start looking for a solution. Now in the simple example of my not being dressed to go out for an ice cream cone in San Antonio, I merely changed my clothes and I had solved the problem and could reach my goal. After I had the ice cream cone, I felt a little less lonely (my love and belonging needs had been partially met). I then had the physiological goal of rest. The problem of inappropriate dress came up again. The double motivation kick in, and I changed clothes and went to bed. The cycle continues forever.

The San Antonio example may be too simplistic. It obviously doesn't take long to figure out that wearing pajamas is not appropriate for the River Walk. But the concept is the same no matter how far away the goal nor how complex the problems.

The concept can be diagrammed:

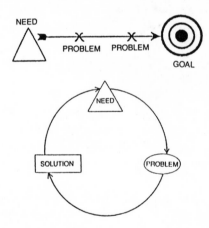

1. We are motivated to reach goals that we feel will meet our Maslow needs.
2. We work toward those goals and encounter a problem.
3. We work on the problem, which creates motivation to solve the problem.
4. The double motivation causes us to change (or buy) in order to solve the problem and get closer to our goal.
5. The cycle continues. Our change brings the solution. We reach that goal and go on to others or we encounter another problem.

Notice that the motivation is internal. People do things for their reasons, not ours. It is *their perception* that reaching certain goals will meet their Maslow needs that counts. It is *their perception* of what the problem is and *their perception* of how to solve that problem that convinces them to act. This concept is critical if we are to understand our role in helping with this process.

So how do we get involved in helping someone go through this process? It may seem like an oversimplification, but the answer is in asking questions, listening, and giving feedback. Here's an example:

Several years ago I hurt my back. I hate to tell you how I hurt it. I was forty-four years old at the time and trying to pretend I was twenty. I was at a picnic at the lake and someone asked if I wanted to water-ski. I said, "Sure." I hadn't been waterskiing in twenty years and was out of shape. but I didn't want to admit that. I went waterskiing, but my back didn't. They say you can tell you're getting older if your back goes out more than you do. I had reached that age.

I had lots of goals and lots of problems. I didn't have time to lie down and wait for my back to get better. So I kept working, traveling, teaching seminars, trying to ignore the pain and hoping it would go away. It didn't. Finally, one night at the supper table, I literally fell out of my chair and crawled to bed. I called my friend Dean Sadler. I was living in Conroe at the time and Dean was the "dean" of the medical community. Dr. Sadler was extremely successful. He took no new patients since managing his clinic, hospital, oil, banking, and other interests took so much of his time. But for those of us who were fortunate enough to be his patients, he even made housecalls.

He said, "Dick, I'm headed to the hospital in a few minutes. I'll drop by."

When he came in the bedroom he did not start talking about solutions. A lot of doctors would have. Most of us think we have to talk about our product or service, our solutions. Dr. Sadler did not. We both knew he had solutions. He wanted to find out about the problem.

If he had started with solutions, such as, "Dick, your back's out. I'm going to put you in the hospital and run these tests and give you such and such therapy," I would not have gone along. I had a seminar in Odessa, Texas, the next weekend, with plans made for thirty-five people, flights scheduled, and a check in the bank. I had to go. I would have said, "Doc, I can't do it. I've got to be in Odessa. Give me some pills, a cane, or whatever. But you've got to get me to Odessa."

Dean didn't start with solutions. He started with my problem. "Tell me what happened."

"Well, I went waterskiing and my back went out. I felt it the minute the boat started to pull me up out of the water."

"Dick, we find that when something like this happens it's been coming on for a while. Can you remember any of these pains before—even to a small extent?

The question caused me to think. "As a matter of fact, I went horseback riding in the mountains on our vacation several weeks ago. When I went out to jog the next morning, I felt a little pain in my leg."

Then he explained to me about backs. He used those words that doctors use with me quite often now, "Dick, as we get older..." He drew a little diagram of my spine. He showed me how the pounding of the horse had exacerbated the problem of a weakened disk. Then he asked if there was anything else.

I said, "Now that you mention it, I went jogging in Nashville several weeks ago. I was staying downtown and the only place I could find was the concrete parking lot around the capitol building. I remember thinking at the time that this was hard on me. I can't remember if I had any pains, though."

Together we were exploring my problem. He was asking questions and mixing my knowledge of my problem with his knowledge of backs. There was an interesting side effect. All of a sudden I was beginning to focus on my goal of good health and solving this immediate problem of the back pain rather than the goal of financial success and Odessa.

Then he asked what side the injury was on. I said, "The *back* side." He laughed. "No. It will be either on the left or the right." I didn't know that.

I was lying on my back. He reached over and lifted my right leg. Nothing. Then he lifted my left leg. The pain shot down my sciatic nerve. I now knew that the injury was on the left side.

Then he said, "Which vertebra is it?" I said, "*All* of them." He laughed again. I think he kept me as a patient for the entertainment value. "No. Turn over. We'll find it." He began pressing on my vertebrae, starting at my neck. When he got down to what I have since learned is the L5, S1 space, he and I both discovered where the injury was located. The pain was excruciating.

Aside from the two of us discovering the details of my problem some other things were going on. For one thing, the importance of Odessa was fading in my mind. The pain in my back, now much more localized, and finding a way to stop it was becoming much more the focus of my attention.

But Dean still wasn't ready to tell me about his solution. He first had to give me what I call a Summary Feedback. Although he had been giving me some feedback all along—some of it no more than a nod—he now summarized our whole conversation. He asked if I thought he understood the problem. I agreed. This Summary Feedback is so important that I devote an entire chapter to it later on. But this part of the story is critical. The Summary Feedback did several things. First, it did what it was intended to do. It made sure that the doctor really had understood the problem. It checked for mistakes. There were also some other more subtle things it accomplished. It further reinforced my focus on the problem— more motivation. Probably the most important thing it accomplished, however, was that it let me know that Dean had heard me and understood me. When someone listens to and understands me I assume they care. It is a way they can let me know they care without telling me they care. By their letting me know they care in this method, I trust not only in their caring but I tend to trust their solution.

Then he said, "Dick, I'm going to put you in the hospital. We'll give you some therapy and run some tests to make sure we know what we're dealing with. But I think we'll have you on your feet in a few days."

I said, "Let's go." I had all but forgotten about Odessa. I called the next day and made other arrangements. What had happened during our conversation was that the doctor's questions had focused my attention on only one of my many goals—good health. And after a thorough discussion of the main problem that was keeping me from reaching that goal, I was motivated to find a solution to that one problem. My other goals and problems faded into the background.

Now I admit that focusing on physical pain is a very simple example of this process. But it is a fact of human nature. If I focus on the pain in lieu of all else, my feelings of pain get worse. There are countless stories of heroes who were in far greater pain than I and yet still were able to save lives or accomplish other incredible feats almost without feeling the pain because their focus was elsewhere.

It almost goes without saying that in your sales situation you are the doctor, the one who knows solutions to certain problems. Your prospect is the patient with problems you can solve. All anyone can hope to do in a sales call is to ask questions to uncover a problem and then together with the prospect explore, define, and examine that problem and help find a solution—hopefully yours. Any other selling is luck, the numbers game, or plain order taking.

I have a client who is in the oil-field-service business, managing oil fields for absentee owners. The company had just decided to get into this line of work at the downturn of the oil boom in the early eighties. They had managed their own fields and had been in related oil-field-service work. Someone suggested they call on a banker. They did. The banker signed them up to manage a field that the bank had just repossessed. My client said the call was easy. "We just walked in and he almost took our proposal out of our hands."

Unfortunately, my client hasn't had many of these "easy" calls since. You see, the banker had already focused on his goal to salvage some money from a sour oil loan. He had studied the problem of what to do with this field that he now owned but knew little about running. My client walked in with the solution. The banker had already gone through the cycle of behavior change to the point of seeking a solution. My client happened in at the right time. Luck!

The numbers game gets credit for a lot of this kind of luck. Just make enough calls and you will get results. There is the great story of the sales manager exhorting his crew to make more calls, make more calls. One day at the weekly report meeting one salesman reported eighty-three calls for the week.

The sales manager said, "Wow! Tell us how you did it."

"It was easy," came the reply. "I could have made even more but a few people asked me what I was selling."

Another story I have heard is supposed to be true. It's about an encyclopedia salesman in Chicago in the 1930s who was consistently the sales leader in the district. The sales manager called him up to the front of a meeting and asked him to tell the others how he did it. Here's what he said:

I live fairly near the downtown section of Chicago, the Loop. Every day I get on the el and go into town. There are a lot of people inside the Loop. I spend all day walking the streets, going in and out of offices [remember there was no air conditioning or security clearances in those days], asking people the same question, "Do you want to buy an encyclopedia?" Most of them say "No." That doesn't take much time. I go on to the next one. I can ask that question of two hundred or three hundred people in a day. But you know, invariably one or two of them will say something like, "Hey. My wife and I were just talking about that the other night. Our kids need an encyclopedia. Maybe it's time we take a look at one." I make an appointment to see them that night, and my sales ratio is pretty high.

That's the numbers game. I personally don't have time to play it. If you do and it works keep it up. But in my selling, and I assume in yours, I have to become like a partner to my client. Part of my ability to sell my solution rests on the prospect's assurance that I understand his problem. That's why my understanding this process and getting involved in it is so important.

So, as we have described above, exploring, defining, and examining a problem increases the prospect's motivation to find a solution. It is also true that in looking closely at a problem one is also focusing on the goal that lies beyond that problem's solution. It is this focus that enhances our prospect's motivation.

Let me add one point in case you might still be suspicious that we are manipulating someone into doing something they don't want to do or buying something they don't want or need. The very fact that I go through this process with you assures that we are dealing with *your* problem and *your* goal. No one will make up a problem or goal just to please me.

But then you say, "Yes, but what about the time I bought something from that salesman who was so pushy I bought something just to get rid of him"—or to please him, if he was charming.

Sure. I did exactly that with a copy machine salesman this past year. But the charming, persistent salesperson had become my problem. I can't say exactly why I bought the copy machine: perhaps to please him, perhaps to get rid of him, or perhaps even so he would not think I was stupid. Boy, was I stupid. The machine made about fifty copies and died. A thirty-day guarantee on a used machine and it died on the fortieth day. I bought another one this year, this time a new one with a two-year guarantee.

In this illustration the salesman had become my problem. I bought the machine in order to solve a problem. But the problem was the salesman and not my original problem. I personally don't want to become my client's problem. But some salespeople think that that is the only way to sell.

The whole process of selling, then, is asking questions, listening for goals and problems, and exploring this with the client. You may have already known that at some level. As we went through this story you may have said, "Yeah. That's what worked so well with Mr. Whoever." But now that we have the process clearly stated, our next problem is to get into the position of asking questions. Let's start looking at some methods that have worked.

4

Why Are You Here?

NOW that you know why people buy something and the part you can play in that process, let's look at how you can set things up to get involved in that process.

I call this the "Call Purpose Statement." It tells the prospect the purpose of your call. It sets the stage that puts you in a position to ask questions and get involved in the prospect's business and ultimately his problems. Remember, if they don't have a problem we don't have a sale.

The Call Purpose Statement is a brief but extremely necessary step in every contact with the prospect. You use it in getting the first appointment. You use it again to structure the first interview. You revise it and use it again on every subsequent call.

Let me give you a few examples of a Call Purpose Statement. In addition to my business of public seminars on selling, our company also does consulting on the development of strategic and marketing plans for small businesses. Often as part of this planning we do market research, sales training, and management training. These are our solutions to specific problems that our clients have. Our ultimate purpose in a call is to uncover these problems and get our prospect to see them, understand them, and want to solve them.

I have a basic Call Purpose Statement that I customize for the particular situation. That situation may vary, based on the type of company on which I'm calling and whether I'm making the call by myself or with someone else. It might also change with each subsequent call I make.

So for this example let's say I am calling on a prospect recommended to me by a current client. It is a company that manufacturers specialized vessels for the petro-chemical industry. My client tells me that this company has developed a method for lining these vessels with various plastics that are highly resistant to corrosion and erosion. My client thinks they might need some help in marketing this new process.

For the sake of this illustration, let's assume that I have already made the appointment and am in the prospect's office. I'll come back and show you how I use a modified version of the Call Purpose Statement to set up an appointment.

At this point I have come into the prospect's office. Let's call him Jim. We shake hands. He offers me a seat. He asks if I had any trouble finding him and I commend him on his clear directions.

I notice a number of industry-award plaques on the wall and comment on them. Jim spends a few minutes telling me about his company's standing in the industry and a little of its history. The company started as a small boat-repair facility in the twenties and got into the vessel-manufacturing business after World War II, when the petro-chemical industry began outfitting for peacetime production. Jim is the company's third president and has been in that position for over ten years. He started working for the company right out of high school.

We now have developed a rapport. That is, we are both comfortable with each other and ready to go to work. Developing rapport is so important that I will spend several chapters on it. Yet in this case it has taken only a couple of minutes.

Now there is a pause in the conversation. We have finished the thought process and it is time to move on to the business at hand. At this point I pretend that Jim is asking me the question "Dick, why are you here?" I have only had one person rude enough to actually ask that question but it is my opinion that every prospect wants me to answer that question at this point in the conversation. The Call Purpose Statement is the answer to that question. So here goes:

Jim, our friend Mark [my client who made the recommendation] tells me that you have an exciting new process that you feel could expand your business considerably, but that was about all he knew about it. He thought I ought to talk to you about it. I don't know how much Mark has told you about us but we are a marketing-consulting firm that has been in business since 1976.

Before that I was a founding officer of Allied Bancshares. You may remember that company. We took a small group of banks and built one of the most successful service companies in the nation.

Anyway, in the years since 1976 I've worked with over four hundred companies, helping them increase profits by developing marketing plans or with our other services, which include strategic planning and sales and management training. You may know that I have been working with Mark's company for the last couple of years. We developed a marketing plan for him, trained several of his key people to make better sales calls, and have continued to work with him in the expansion of his business.

To be perfectly honest, I've never worked for a firm that makes pressure vessels. Most of my work has been with companies that sell products or services to other companies, and I feel like the basics of marketing would probably apply to your business, too. But I don't know for sure. I find that the best way for me to know if I might be of help to you is to learn as much as I can about your company, where you've been, what you do, who you do it for, and how you have marketed yourself in the past. Then I think I could present what we do in a way that makes sense to you in your specific market. So it would help if you just tell me something about your business and this new process you have. You've already told me a little about the history. Why don't you tell me a little about what you do and who you do it for?

That is the Call Purpose Statement. It takes less than two minutes to go through, but it is a powerful tool in setting the stage for me to get involved in the prospect's life and ultimately his problems. It obviously has been customized to fit the prospect that makes pressure vessels. However, if you heard me give my Call Purpose Statement to a dozen clients you would see that the basics are about the same. There is a brief introduction of my company and what we do along with my personal work history, my credentials. There is a list of our services and a broad brush about the companies I've worked for. Depending on the response and the prospect I might elaborate on a few of my clients, giving names and types of business. But I say very little about my business. I don't want to talk about that at this point.

The next basic element is to give a reason for learning about the prospect's business. The prospect wants to know what we are going to accomplish during our visit and what the procedure will be. I have given all of that in the two-minute Call Purpose Statement.

There is one other critical element. I have asked for his help. You might have noticed that I said, "It would help me if..." Four of the most powerful words in the English language are, "I need your help." People like to help, particularly if they can help by talking about their own business. Asking for help is a statement of humility. It is appealing. By the way, in my case it is also sincere humility. At the beginning of this call I didn't know much at all about the pressure-vessel business. I needed help.

Humility is powerful. Most people do not expect salespeople to be humble. It is fresh and attractive. Are these words familiar? "The world will little note, nor long remember, what we say here, but it can never forget what they did here." That speech ends with "and that government of the people, by the people, for the people, shall not perish from the earth." Who knows why Lincoln's Gettysburg address is one of the most memorized pieces of American history? There seems little doubt, though, that its underlying humility has something to do with its appeal.

The problem with humility, of course, is that it is hard to do on purpose. A sincere recognition of a need for help, of your inability to know everything, is a beginning. Try it.

Notice, too, that I have told him he could help by talking about his business. In my experience almost everyone likes to talk about his business. In the past I have called on people who started in their garage and have built a multimillion-dollar business. Their spouse won't let them brag at the bridge club. Then I come in, have a certain amount of credibility, seem trustworthy, and I'm asking them to brag to me about their business. Usually my problem after the Call Purpose Statement is getting people to shut up. Once they get started—and I show interest in what they are saying—they don't want to quit.

Now here is the key element of the Call Purpose Statement. I have told the prospect what work I am asking him to do. He wants me to do that. I have asked for the meeting and he wants me to direct its course. I have set the stage now for him to tell me about his business, for me to listen, ask questions, and listen for goals and problems.

Another key factor in the Call Purpose Statement is what I have *not* told him. I have not told him that I'm here to sell him something. Most people don't like to be "sold" something. If I had said, "Jim, the reason I'm here is to sell you my services," I would have lost the rapport that I had spent time developing.

"But," you say, "you *are* there to sell him something. He will know that and see through your charade." No. The truth is, at this point, I don't know whether I have something to sell him or not. I don't know enough about his business to know whether or not I can help. I don't know what he is trying to accomplish (his goals). I don't know what problems are keeping him from reaching those goals. So I sure don't know if I have the right solution to those problems. He will have to help me learn that. I am now in a true consultant's role. Together he and I will develop an understanding of his goals and problems so that we can together determine if he has a problem he thinks I can solve. Honesty is critical. I must truly believe in this role as a consultant or my dishonesty will show and a key factor in the process, trust, will be lost.

In truth, I don't want to sell him something that he does not want or need. The worst thing that can happen to my business as a marketing consultant is selling a solution that I can't produce or that won't solve the problem.

Thomas Peters and Robert Waterman, in their book *In Search of Excellence,* state that the second of eight principles used in the country's best-run companies is "staying close to the customer— learning his preferences and catering to them."

I work a lot with banks, since that was my background. Bankers have a problem with this concept of not selling something until they're sure they have the right solution. They will say things like, "He knows I'm trying to sell him something. Otherwise, why would I be out at his office. Why would I have called him?"

Then I ask the bankers what happens if they get a prospect to move his business to their bank against his will. The answer, of course, is, "We have an unhappy customer who leaves us at the first opportunity. Or worse yet, we get a loan that is never paid back." So, you see, they certainly don't want to sell somebody something until both parties are certain that the marriage will be a good one. The same can probably be said about your business. Try it out.

Here is another example. This is one we developed for the

company that leases temporary office space. In writing a marketing plan for this company we found that the sales staff was
spending 80 percent of their sales time on the phone trying to lease
construction-office trailers. Of the three market segments the
company services this was the most competitive, the hardest to sell,
and the least profitable. In our studies we found that even though
the sales staff was spending 80 percent of their time selling this
product, primarily by following up on information from a construction reporting service over 80 percent of their sales came from
current or past customers. They were spinning their wheels.

We suggested that the salespeople spend most of their time out of
the office making sales calls. The calls were the best way to sell
their more profitable office complexes, which leased for much
higher rates and usually stayed in place for over three years. In
addition, the personal calls were a good way to further cement
relationships with the repeat customers that were leasing most of
the trailers.

We identified a number of industries that were prime prospects
for the office complexes. Among these was the hospital industry.
Many hospitals have construction programs under way or planned.
Because most of these projects are extensions of existing buildings,
the construction often displaces a number of the office staff,
sometimes for two years or more. With a little research we found
that hospital administrators were largely unaware that first-class
office space could be moved into their current parking lot and
attached to the present building. Many of these administrators
would look for vacant office space nearby in existing office
buildings. Seldom is this space very close to the hospital, and the
separation creates tremendous problems for management. The
cost, too, is often high, and most office-building landlords require
longer leases than the hospitals are willing to commit to. The office
complexes are an ideal solution. Sales calls are the ideal way to
educate the hospital administrators and sell the complexes.

The company had rented a 40,000-square-foot complex almost by
accident to a major hospital in a major city. The administrator had
been looking at vacant office space near the hospital. He could not
find adequate space less than a mile from the hospital. The
logistics would be a nightmare. He anticipated using the space for
two to three years. There was a possibility of another construction

project following the current one, which could extend the need for space to four or five years. He just happened to read an article in a hospital journal about a hospital up North that had used temporary office complexes. He called our firm and found the solution.

The replacement of office space for over forty employees required nine units of the premanufactured complexes to be joined together. Though this is usually easily accomplished, the roof joints in this particular complex were somewhat faulty and the hospital had problems with leaks for several months after the installation. However, our people were very attentive and their efforts to fix the problem finally paid off. Their responsiveness was appreciated. In fact the administrator was so pleased with the offices and the service he had received that he recommended our company to two other hospitals that subsequently leased space. We were in the business and wanted more.

We decided to make a concerted effort to call on all the hospitals in the markets we served. Finding the people on whom to call was the easy part. The hospital industry is quite small and there are directories readily available that list the administrators. For this reason we decided not to wait until a hospital announced a construction project. For one thing, that would probably be too late. Administrators will make arrangements for their people's relocation well in advance of a formal announcement. For another thing, we felt that we had to provide an education for hospital administrators and that even those not anticipating construction would still find the problem/solution stories of their peers interesting.

In addition, we had a very high profile hospital as a customer. The name itself would give us entrée to many administrators' offices.

So here was our strategy. Our main objective was to get information from the hospital administrator about plans for the future. Our secondary objective was to educate that administrator on our building product as a solution to construction problems. Of course, our first objective was to get an interview.

So we developed a Call Purpose Statement that we thought would accomplish our goals. We would then use the essence of that Call Purpose Statement to get the interview.

Here was the statement: "Mr. Administrator, our reason for asking for this interview was twofold. First, we have helped High

Profile Hospital solve a major problem in their construction program—where to put displaced office workers for the two- or three-
year program. Mr. Administrator at High Profile Hospital had tried
finding office space in the area and was faced with placing his
people some two to three miles away. Our buildings were custom-
designed and installed on the parking lot adjacent to his present
building.

"We think this solution might be helpful to other hospitals in the
future, but if we are going to gear our company to be ready to help
when a project like this comes up we are going to have to know
more about the hospitals in this area and the general trends in the
industry as a whole and your hospital in particular. It would really
help me if you told me a little about your hospital, your job here, and
what you see in the future."

After we got the opening then we were ready with a number of
questions about this hospital's patient load, market, past growth,
projected future growth, ownership, financing, and so on.

We then took a shorter version of the Call Purpose Statement
and used it on the phone to get the interview. Our work with the
high profile hospital helped us a lot, of course, in getting the
interview. Everyone was curious about what their peers were up to
and thought they might learn something from talking to us.

Granted we were more successful at getting interviews with
those administrators who had construction projects in mind, even
if they weren't ready to talk about them. But this, too, helped us get
before a better-qualified prospect.

I use a similar version of the Call Purpose Statement for every
call. There are times, of course, when I am calling on a person who
has already expressed interest in one of our services. I still want to
back up and get involved with the prospect in his total situation and
goals. I want to get his perspective on his problem and why he
thinks our service will solve it.

Remember the double motivation brought about by focusing on
both the specific goal and that goal's problem or problems? The
more the prospect talks about his goals and problems the more apt
he is to want a solution. Besides, my solution may not be right for
the problem. One of our other services might be better. I won't
know this unless I understand what my prospect is trying to

accomplish (the goal) and what problems are keeping him from reaching that goal.

A banker called me the other day to say he wanted me to present my selling-skills seminar to his loan officers. "How much would that cost?" he asked.

I could have quoted the price for our basic training, maybe sold it, but I would not really have helped the banker with his problem and I would have missed a much larger sale. Instead I said, "We've got a lot of approaches to training bank officers how to sell. I think if I could sit down with you and find out what your officers are doing now and what you want them to do, and learn a little more about your bank I would be in a better position to tell you which one of our courses would best suit your needs. Would you have a few minutes to visit with me if I come by?"

The banker agreed and we set up a time. When I arrived at his bank I was really impressed with the bright colors and open spaces—no dark wood or somber, cramped offices. This gave me an opening for the rapport development. When I asked him about it he lit up. Apparently he had always hated dark, formal-looking banks and the colors and openness were his idea to make customers feel more comfortable.

After a few minutes of discussing the décor we both relaxed, and then there was the pause. He wanted to know why I was here, what we would do with our time together. Granted he made the first contact but I was the one who suggested we get together. He was looking to me to direct the interview. It was time for the Call Purpose Statement.

"Well, Mr. Banker, I appreciate your taking time to see me. You had called and asked about our sales training. I find that usually when I get a call like that, a banker is having problems getting a sales-call program off the ground or in some other way is dissatisfied with what his calling officers are doing.

"We have lots of ways of helping with these problems. But I find that the more I know about your bank and what your goals are the better able I am to see which of our methods might be the most helpful. So it would help me a lot if you just gave me some background on where you are."

And we were off and running on a call that lasted over an hour.

As it turned out the bank had many problems in the area of getting its officers out to make calls. They needed much more than just the training seminar. As a result of this call I was able to propose a total program that would help them achieve their goals. My fee was about four times what it would have been for the seminar alone.

Now let's look at how we use the Call Purpose Statement to get our first appointment. I mentioned that we use a version of the Call Purpose Statement over the phone on the first contact.

Let's go back to the first call that I made on the pressure-vessel manufacturing firm. As I said, he had been recommended to me by another client. We'll talk about prospecting in a later chapter. But one thing I will say is that your best prospect is one recommended by a mutual acquaintance. I always call these prospects first. They have the highest priority. I, of course, mention this recommendation in my first phone call and as an introduction in the first interview (provided I have permission from my contact). In this case the phone conversation went something like this:

Mr. Prospect, I have been working with Mark Stephens for the last couple of years in helping him develop a workable marketing program. He may have mentioned us to you. (I pause here to get his response. If he says, "Yes" and has any comments I follow up on that. If he says, "No" I continue.) Well, Mark mentioned to me his friendship with you and has shared with me a little about your business. He was excited about your new process for lining vessels with plastics and your thought that there is a large market for this new service. He thought I should talk to you about our services.

(At this point the prospect will usually either verify my statement or clarify it if need be. I respond to his comments and continue.)

My firm has been in business since 1976. We've been helping companies like yours solve problems of marketing, and it sounds like we might have some solutions for your current situation. I've worked with some four hundred companies like yours in helping them expand their markets.But to be honest, I have never worked for a company exactly like yours. While we may have some answers for you it would help me present our services in a more meaningful manner if I could visit with your for awhile and learn more about your business. Would you have some time next week for me to come by and meet with you?

It is a short version of the Call Purpose Statement. It piques the prospect's interest, particularly if he has been wrestling with the problem of marketing his new product, which this prospect had been doing. I got the appointment.

In the case of the temporary office space salespeople, the telephoned Call Purpose Statement was a little different. It went something like this:

> Mr. Administrator, we are the company that provided temporary office space for High Profile Hospital. Mr. Jones, the administrator for High Profile, has been extremely pleased with our solution to his problem. In fact, so much so that he has recommended us to Blank Hospital and Blank Hospital. We are installing buildings there, too. Have you seen any of these installations? (Again, we pause here, wait for a response and respond to it. Then we continue.) Because of our experience with these three hospitals we feel that our service might be particularly helpful to the hospital business in general. However, to be sure that we have our company geared to serving the hospital market we feel it is imperative that we talk to as many administrators as we can to make sure we are geared to meet the particular needs of this special market. Consequently we are endeavoring to visit with people like you just to learn about your business and how you see your needs. So I wonder if you could take a few minutes for me to come by and ask you a few questions about your hospital and what you see as the future for your hospital in particular and the hospital industry as a whole.

We, of course, did not get an appointment with everyone we called. However, we did get a pretty high percentage, and often those we did get in to see were considering a construction project in the near future. Often we didn't find that out until later.

So, whether we were trying to get the first interview or were setting the stage after we got that interview, the Call Purpose

Statement was an invaluable part of setting the stage for gaining a consultative role with our prospect.

In fact, if the Call Purpose Statement is done correctly we are almost forced to make a good call. The worst that can happen to us after that is that we learn a lot about a prospect and an industry for which we have solutions, information that will be invaluable to us at some point in the future.

5

Howdy Doody Wasn't All Wrong

R APPORT DEVELOPMENT. Everybody knows you have to develop rapport with a prospect. Right? Probably so. But I am sometimes amazed at how inept some people are at this when they are out making calls. It is as though the call is so foreign to them that they forget all of their interpersonal skills.

In the last chapter and in previous chapters I demonstrated that rapport development can take less than a couple of minutes. It seems almost insignificant. But without it—now hear this—we not only could not make a sale, we could not even have the interview.

We all develop rapport with other people. We have a ritual of rapport development every morning when we greet our spouse. It may be a grunt or a groan. It may be a cheery, "Good morning!" But it is our way of reestablishing rapport in the family.

At the office we have little rituals of rapport development. We talk about the game or the party the night before. There is little chitchat that reestablishes our relationship as human beings.

Do you remember a time in your office where Mr. or Ms. Cheery, who always had a smile and a warm greeting, came in one morning with a scowl, walked right to his or her office, and closed the door. What happened to productivity that morning? Unless you have a unique office, everything stopped until you found out what was wrong with Mr./Ms. Cheery.

Or has the opposite happened? The crotchety one, who always has a sour look and never speaks in the morning, comes in singing and cheery. Wow! Everything stops until we find out what has happened—or worse—what is going to happen.

Rapport development is a part of our lives. We are constantly reassuring each other that we, too, are human. We are alike. We think, feel, laugh, cry, hurt, enjoy in much the same way. One dictionary defines *rapport* as a harmonious and understanding relationship between people. Remember from our chapter on the loyal customer how important understanding is in a synergistic relationship.

But as expert as we all are in developing personal rapport, many with whom I've worked seem to leave all of these skills behind when making a call. I think there are several good reasons for that.

One, if we have been in a business in which people have come to us with their problems, like banking, architecture, engineering, medicine, or accounting, then we have let the client or customer do the rapport development. They are on our turf. They will usually take on the role of rapport developer.

Think about some of your clients. When you first met them, did they not comment on your furnishings, plaques, the weather, or in some other way open the rapport-development business?

Back in my banking days I had a friend who was in the advertising business. He had long curly hair and usually wore open shirts, gold chains, the works for the "in" guy at the time. Once I saw him in a three-piece dark suit with white shirt and tie.

I said, "What's this?" pointing to the obvious differences.

He said, "Oh, this is my banker's suit. I'm here to see about extending my loan. These bankers like dark suits." Then he quickly added, "Not you, of course. You're marketing."

But the point is that people will change themselves to develop rapport with us if they are coming to us to solve their problems. The big difference in making a call is that the shoe is on the other foot. We are on their turf. We have asked for their time. We want them to solve our problems. We are responsible for developing the rapport.

A major problem in rapport development is what I call "relationship tension." Understanding this very common human problem is critical to developing rapport on the other person's turf.

I'll start with a simple example. How many times have you been introduced to someone and realized only a few minutes later that you could not recall their name. The reason for that is relationship tension.

At the beginning of seminars I usually go around the room and have everyone introduce themselves and tell a little about their background. I give everyone a series of simple and unthreatening questions to answer. Occasionally, to illustrate this point about the negative power of relationship tension, I will ask them to tell me what the person just ahead of them said. Most people can't do it. They are so busy worrying about what they are going to say when it is their turn that they can't let any data in from the outside.

Going back to the first-time introduction, the reason we can remember their name after a few minutes of conversation is that we have developed rapport by then, reduced the relationship tension. At that time another kind of tension sets in—task tension. (Some might argue that this is really a difference in the amount of the same kind of tension rather than a difference in kind, but for illustration purposes I find it helpful to label them as different kinds of tension.)

We all have to have tension. We can't get out of bed without tension. There is tension between the muscles whenever we lift a finger, wave our hand, or pick up a book. We can't walk without tension. We can't talk without tension. We sure can't work or think without it. Tension is good. But relationship tension is damaging and we need to understand it and learn to remove it in both ourselves and others. We can illustrate the difference between relationship tension and task tension this way:

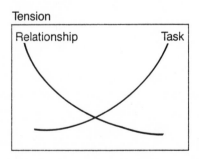

In the model above, Tension is on the vertical axis and Rapport is on the horizontal axis. As we develop rapport (move to the right of the model) Relationship Tension drops and Task Tension increases.

Part of the dynamic operating here is that it is human nature for people to want to go to work when their relationship tension drops.

Now the task or work tension may be in the form of play. You may take a group of strangers out to the lake to go waterskiing. They will stand around on the beach for a little while asking questions about where the others went to school, what kind of music they like, and such. Then when the relationship tension has dropped sufficiently someone will say, "Hey, didn't we come out here to water-ski? Let's get in the boat." If two or more people develop rapport enough to have task tension rise they will always want to go to work.

At this point you may say something like, "Dick, I've got some people I work with that you haven't met yet."

Granted we all know a "bum," that guy who never wants to work. He can't hold a job, is never productive. But if you really think about it, that person, for one reason or another, has a problem that keeps his relationship tension high no matter what you do. He's mad at his father, God, society, or whatever. But for some reason his relationship tension can't be brought down. You have seen some of these same people who have gotten close to a counselor, minister, or someone who has found the key to their anger and solved it. These people then become productive citizens. It is important that we know this rule of human nature. Develop rapport with me, a friend, your fellow workers, your prospect, and that person will always want to go to work.

Now let's look at the behaviors exhibited when one is feeling task tension. They are cooperative, problem solving, and creative. We tend to think of creativity as having to do with the arts, music, or drama. But all work is basically problem solving and problem solving requires creativity. So we all are creative when we are productive.

Now let's look at the behavior people exhibit when their relationship tension is high. Their focus is on themselves. They are self-conscious, focused inward. They may be quiet, somber. Or some may be loud and boisterous. Some tell jokes, but even these jokes have an angry, cutting-edge to them. Others are pushy, trying to exert their will on someone else. All of this behavior has one purpose; it is defensive. The very word is a military term. We throw up the ramparts to keep the enemy out. In football we have a defensive line. That line's purpose is to keep the other team out of our end of the field.

The purpose of the defensive behavior is the same; to keep

others out, to block them from hurting us. I'm sure you've had the experience of having someone come into your office with a problem. They are tense, their relationship tension is high. You look at the problem and show them exactly how to solve it. Then the next words out of their mouth tell you that they have not heard a word you have said. Their defensive wall was there to keep you out and it worked so well they couldn't even hear the words you were saying even though you had solved their problem.

It is pretty obvious at this point that we must have our prospects and ourselves on the task-tension side of the model if we are going to accomplish anything in our call. Remember we said that no one buys anything from us unless they have a problem they think we can solve. Problem solving is work, or a task. So our task tension has to be high, we have to be cooperative and creative, if we want to accomplish anything in our call. So it's easy to see that rapport development is an absolute necessity if we are to be successful in finding and defining our prospect's problem in order for us to present our solution.

Now that you see the value of rapport development, that we must reduce our own and the prospect's relationship tension, you may see another problem. It is often difficult to tell when a person's relationship tension is high. As adults we have learned to cover our emotions. We don't always give clear signs of high relationship tension.

This is particularly true in the seminars I give. I have to spend some time reducing the group's relationship tension or the seminar will be a flop. No one will hear what I have to say. In small groups of fifteen to twenty-five I usually go around the room and have everyone introduce themselves, tell their name, their job, something about their company. Usually for fun I also ask them to tell where they were born and reared. One seminar leader I know asks her participants to tell how their childhood home was heated. The idea is to get people focusing on something fairly nonthreatening to get their focus off themselves and to relate to others as human beings, rapport development. On the few occasions when I have skipped this part of the seminar, I have faced some rather difficult groups.

My relationship tension is always rather high when I first start a seminar with people I don't know. I have a lot of pressure to perform. I want to be successful. I want these people to like me, learn from me, appreciate me, hire me for other work. If I'm not successful in the seminar, word will get around. I'll be out of work.

In many of the courses I teach I use this model for understanding defensiveness and the need for rapport development. I usually introduce it after the seminar is going well and it is obvious that task tension has set in. I explain some of the pressures I was feeling when the seminar started. I ask the participants how they would have felt had they been me when I first started the seminar. They all agree that they would have felt some relationship tension. I admit that I did. Then I ask them how many of them spotted it in me. Almost no one ever says they saw it. I'm a professional. I should be able to cover it up.

The truth of the matter is that most of us have developed ways that cover our relationship tension. At that point I ask the participants how many of them—not knowing me, not knowing the other participants, not knowing exactly what was expected of them—felt relationship tension at the beginning. Invariably, most of them hold up their hands. I then give them some feedback; they didn't show it either. I could no more tell that they were tense than they could tell that I was. And so we demonstrate the difficulty in spotting relationship tension. We all hide it so well.

Now, granted, if you know someone well you can pick up on the nervous behavior: the higher-pitched voice, the too-easy laughter that characterizes that person's relationship tension. But we are talking about your making a call on a stranger, or at least someone who has never been in this call situation with you before. How do we spot the relationship tension? How do we know when it is gone and that task tension is sufficiently high to go to work?

There are two guidelines that I use to tell me when relationship tension is present. These are guidelines, by the way, and not rules. They are to be used cautiously and mixed with other guidelines.

The first: Whenever there is something new between two or more people there will probably be some relationship tension. In my seminars there is always something new. I'm new to the group. Members of the group are new to each other. The subject matter is new. The group, at least in this context, is new to me.

When you go out to call on a prospect there is something new. You don't know each other. They don't know your company. You don't know their company, their problems, their style, their reactions. The newness is pretty obvious. There will nearly always be relationship tension.

But say you have three employees that have shared an office together, they've worked together maybe for years. They know each other's families. They can almost read each other's minds. Then one Friday afternoon you tell one of them that you are making their threesome a department and you name one of them the manager. Do you think that on Monday there will be some relationship tension? Of course. Because something new has been introduced to the group.

Let's say then that you have a customer or client of long standing. They have always come to your place of business. Now you call them for the first time and tell them you would like to come call on them at their business. Do you think there will be some relationship tension? Of course. Again, something new has been introduced. Rapport development is critical.

The second guideline is based on the fact that defensiveness begets defensiveness. If you are defensive I will intuitively know it and throw up my own defenses. The guideline is: Whenever you feel relationship tension, the chances are that I will feel it, too, and vice versa. So I can read your defensiveness or relationship tension by feeling my own. One of the difficulties with making use of this guideline is that if I'm feeling relationship tension my focus is on me and it is hard for me to focus on you enough to even realize your tension. It can be done, though, with practice.

Oddly enough, if I train myself to think of you when I feel relationship tension, I have begun to turn my focus away from myself and have started the process of reducing my own relationship tension. As defensiveness begets defensiveness, so task tension begets task tension. And so I have taken the first step in developing rapport and getting on with the work at hand.

I'll give you an example of the second guideline. I was teaching a selling-skills course to a group of bankers in Midland, Texas. As the first morning wore on I began to feel tension. My nervousness increased instead of decreased. I started thinking about how to get out of there, when my plane would leave. These are sure signs of my relationship tension. I tried to ignore it. I stayed with the material hoping the tension would subside. It did not. Finally, it got so bad that I stopped right in the middle of a sentence and said, "Say. It may be my imagination but I'm feeling a lot of tension in the room. Have I said something that offended someone?"

Immediately the room broke into laughter. Someone quickly pointed out that I was calling Charles "George." As I looked back, every time I said "George" the tension got worse. When I stopped and asked about it we all had a good laugh, I apologized to Charles, and we got on with the work.

As I mentioned, my relationship tension tends to make me think in terms of leaving, avoiding the situation, getting through with the encounter. You may experience the same symptoms or yours may be different. Basically we have four ways of dealing with relationship tension. See if you recognize yours:

1. Avoidance. That's mine. I want to leave. I remind myself of when my plane takes off. I find a way to leave. I ask for more information. I beg time to study the problem. I use all the other tricks I've learned for avoiding the source of my tension.

2. Becoming dictatorial. Some people start barking orders. They know they can straighten everything out if only everybody will obey. They get loud, pushy, look people in the eye and tell them what to do. If the situation does not allow this behavior, then they feel like doing that and wish that they could.

3. Attacking. Some people lash out at the source of the tension. They go for the juguler. They discuss your ancestry, cast aspersions on your parents' marriage vows, use biblical terms out of context.

4. Acquiescence. These people feel that if they just tell you what they think you want to hear you will go away or at least like them and quit causing the relationship tension. They'll say things like, "You're so smart. I know you're right. You always are, you know. I just admire you so much. Of course we'll do it your way." Of course, they have no intention of doing it your way but that's beside the point. They're like punching a marshmallow. There is no resistance.

These are, of course, generalizations, but most of us can identify with one or more of them. The next time you find yourself with these feelings tell yourself that you are feeling relationship tension. Picture the model. The clinical nature of the exercise may in itself make you laugh and relieve some of your tension. Then see if you can uncover the reason for tension in the other person. What is their problem? How can you help? If you can get that far you will have gone a long way toward reducing the relationship tension and be on your way to task tension and a productive encounter.

This has been a long discussion about a relatively short part of the call, the rapport-development step. I have said that it should take no more than two or three minutes. It may take much less than that. But without it we stay on the defensive, relationship-tension side of the model and nothing gets done.

There are a number of ways to develop rapport. I've given some examples and will give more in the section about typical calls later in the book. A few general guidelines include checking out the environment. What magazines are on the coffee table in the waiting area? *Field and Stream* is a dead giveaway for an outdoors person. Golfing, gardening, auto-racing magazines are all clues. Industry-specific magazines or newsletters are also informative. It means the prospect keeps up. If you have waiting time, read through one of the newsletters. Pick up on some key issues.

There are plaques, pictures, awards. There is the new building or new furnishings. Most people surround themselves with symbols of their interests. Find one you can relate to.

Of course, sporting events, weather, family, and so on are all springboards for developing rapport. However, be honest. Pretending an interest you don't have will be obvious and instead of reducing relationship tension will increase it.

I personally don't play golf. To tell the truth I really think of golf as a way to mess up a good walk. But a lot of my clients and prospects play golf. They often have trophies in their offices indicating they probably spend too much time on the course. If I pretend to be a golfer and go on and on about the trophies, that lie will become obvious. However, I do understand winning. I am competitive. I have played enough golf to know that when you're walking down the fairway having just hit a ball 200 yards straight toward the green you are not thinking about your desk and the work you have to do. Golf is therapeutic. I understand this. So I can say, with honesty, "Tell me about all these trophies. You must be pretty good."

Back in my early days of selling I didn't know about this need for honesty. I walked into a man's office who had a huge sailfish mounted over his credenza.

Now if you have a stuffed sailfish in your possession please skip over this part. I have to be honest in order to make the point. I really don't care much for people who stuff sailfish. In my experience most of them have hired a professional staff who took them offshore in a fancy boat. They usually drank beer while the staff took the boat to where they knew the fish would be. The staff helped bring in the fish and did most of the work. In addition, I have found that the stuffed fish is really plastic and the bright color is airplane dope. The fish turns black the minute he is clubbed to death by the hired staff.

Anyway, I looked up at this man's stuffed fish and said, "Wow. That's quite a fish. Tell me about that."

With a grunt he glanced over his shoulder at the fish and said, "That? I got drunk on a boat in Acapulco. After doing everything for me but reeling in the line those bastards appealed to my vanity, talked me into spending a fortune to have that thing stuffed, and my wife won't let me keep it at home. Now. What can I do for you?"

So much for honesty in developing rapport. By the way, I often relate that story in my selling-skills seminars. One bank had hired me to teach the course and then to make joint calls with some of their younger officers. One young lady with whom I was calling had commented in a couple of calls about my ability to relax people so easily. On the very next call we walked into a man's office who had a huge stuffed sailfish on his wall. My partner leaned over and whispered, "Let's see you get out of this one."

Fortunately the fellow had a framed set of sailor's knots on the wall next to where I sat. I'm a sailor so I asked him about those and ignored the fish for a minute. It turned out that he was an avid sports fisherman and had his own boat and worked hard in sailfishing tournaments. My feelings were a little different about his fish.

One other note of caution about rapport development. As I work with nonselling professionals in making their first calls I find an interesting phenomenon takes place with many of them. Once they get comfortable with rapport development that is all they do. I can almost hear their subconscious mind saying, "Now that I finally know what to say after I say hello, I'm going to keep saying it until it's time to go."

This is what we call the Howdy Doody call. We introduce ourselves, give them our card, tell them a little about our company, find that they share our interest in fishing (camping, football, kids in school), and we're off and running. Thirty minutes later we're still talking about the fishing and it's time for our prospect to go. We excuse ourselves, tell the prospect how much we've enjoyed our little visit and say, "If we can ever be of help to you let us know."

We go to the car, glad that the ordeal is over, feeling a bit proud that we were able to keep the conversation going. But there is a nagging feeling in the pit of our stomachs that the whole episode has been a waste of time. It has. This feeling alone will ensure that you will eventually quit calling and will again wait behind your desk or counter and hope the clients call you.

Perhaps now you would like to tell me that you can develop rapport easily with some people but with others it is hard to do. You are not alone. Most people have this problem. We just relate to some people more easily than others. Earlier I showed you four ways that people express their relationship tension: avoidance, dictatorial, attacking, and acquiescence. We tend to relate more easily to those people who react the same way we do. This reaction comes from our interpersonal style. Understanding how different styles affect our relationships is the subject of the next chapter. Learning to read others' styles will go a long way in helping us develop rapport with a broader range of people.

6

Personal Style: The Language of Difference

WOULDN'T it be nice if people wore a sign around their necks that said, IF YOU TREAT ME _____! WE WILL GET ALONG FINE. This would be especially true when we make a call on them for the first time.

People don't wear signs but their behavior does tell us how to treat them. If I walk into your office, I can tell immediately if you are like me and I can "just be myself." If you are very different from me, I can also determine what your style is pretty easily and therefore have some pretty accurate guidelines as to how I will have to behave in order to make you feel comfortable.

Sounds like magic, doesn't it? No, it is just human nature. We all have developed certain behaviors that express our personal style, our fears, and our needs. Read my behavior and you know my fears and needs. This chapter presents some basic theories of understanding human nature that will serve us well as we examine the other steps in selling.

This concept is not new. Aristotle discussed the sixteen personality types. The TRACOM Corporation in Denver, Colorado, has studied almost a million people to determine their behavioral style.

Their basic premise is that there are four basic interpersonal styles. Each style has its own needs and fears. If you can read my style then you will know what my needs and fears are. You can learn to read behavior to identify interpersonal styles in a broad sense. Once you have identified the style then there are guidelines you can use to affect a better relationship.

It has been my experience as a manager and a consultant that if you understand people's fears you can determine how to work out problems with them. All problems seem to stem from someone's fear. In the last chapter we discussed the four ways that people express their relationship tension. We could say that these are the ways they express their fears. But fear is the negative side of style. Let's first look at the positive side.

Before we do that let me give you a warning. Any time you try to put people in boxes you are asking for trouble. These are guide-lines, not rules. About the time I think I have you figured out and know how to predict your behavior, chances are, you'll change.

But understanding styles can be very helpful in building rela-tionships. It can be extremely helpful in opening a relationship and getting it off on the right foot. Learning to read style is not difficult. For instance, you've probably had the experience of meeting someone for the first time and knowing right away how you'll feel about him: "I'm really gonna like that guy," or "I ain't gonna like this turkey." Did you ever wonder how you knew that? You were reading behavior, or style. You already know how.

Let me first give you an overview of where we're going. There are really only three aspects of behavior that we read. People use these three aspects in combination to express their style.

The most visible aspect of behavior is assertiveness. You may have positive or negative feelings about this word but set those aside for a while. We will soon learn that there are positive and negative aspects to all of the styles and all of the behaviors. Every-one can picture an assertive person. Let's call that person "telling assertive." In your own mind get a picture of the most telling assertive person you know. Now picture the least assertive person you know. Let's call him or her "ask assertive."

Now if we put those two at opposite ends of a horizontal axis we have half of our equation:

"Ask Assertive"——————— | ———————"Tell Assertive"

People tend to be distributed evenly along this continuum of behavior. They tend to fall at many different points along the scale.

But usually we can determine whether a person's behavior is to the left or right of middle.

Now to form the second axis in TRACOM's model we have a behavioral theme we call "responsiveness." Do I show my emotions in my behavior or am I poker-faced? Again, picture the most poker-faced person you know. It doesn't matter whether they are assertive or nonassertive or in between. He just happens to be very closed, not showing his emotions, cool, aloof. We call people like this emotionally "controlled."

Now the opposite. Think of people who are totally open. If they're sad they cry. If they are happy they laugh. They smile easily. They are warm and friendly. If we put these people at the other end of our responsiveness scale we call them "emoting."

Therefore we put emotionally controlled people at the top of this axis and we put the emoting people at the bottom of the axis.

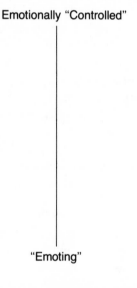

If we overlap the two axes we get four quadrants that represent the four basic Social Style[SM] behaviors:

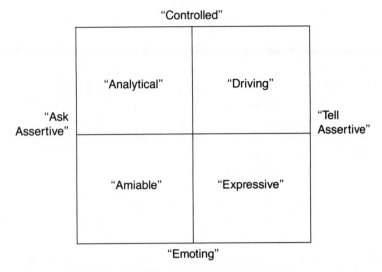

"Controlled"

| "Analytical" | "Driving" |
| "Amiable" | "Expressive" |

"Ask Assertive"   "Tell Assertive"

"Emoting"

The Social Style^SM Model used by permission*

In the upper right quadrant we have the assertive, emotionally controlled behavior that defines a dominant, direct, and outgoing style we'll call the "driving" style.

The lower right is the emoting, tell assertive behavior that defines a people-oriented, dynamic style we'll call the "expressive" style.

Coming around clockwise we find the lower left quadrant represents the ask assertive, emoting behavior that defines a relationship-oriented, easygoing person we'll call the "amiable" style.

Our last quadrant, the upper left, is the ask assertive, emotionally controlled person called the "analytical" style.

Again, let me stress that no two people are exactly alike. We are looking for guidelines, and therefore getting someone loosely situated in one quadrant is all that is necessary to give us a general feel for how to treat him.

---

*The SOCIAL STYLE™ MODEL and the SOCIAL STYLE^SM concepts are a result of the original research of The TRACOM Corporation. All rights reserved. References to the SOCIAL STYLE concepts in this work are used with permission, although certain conclusions regarding SOCIAL STYLE behaviors are the author's and not necessarily supported by TRACOM's research.

Now, let's see if we can learn to read the styles of others. To do this we have to become aware of people's behaviors. Most of us are almost unaware of behavior because we learn early on in life to make judgments about what the behavior means. For instance, let's say I have my arms open wide to you. You would probably interpret that to mean, "Welcome. I'm glad to see you."

If, on the other hand, I have my arms folded, one fist up to my chin, and a stern look on my face, you would probably judge that I was not accepting of you or your idea, that I had to study your proposal.

These judgments would probably be right, but that's not the point. In order to learn to read people's behavior you have to "see" their behavior and postpone making judgments about what it means. In the examples above the behaviors were the open arms, the crossed arms, the fist to the face, and the stern look. That was the behavior. That behavior tells you something about my style, which goes beyond the immediate meaning or judgment.

So when we discuss behavior we basically mean body language (arm and leg movement, stance, etc.), facial expression, including eye contact, tone and volume of voice, and the words we use. This is the "reading" material that people show us so that we will know something about them. The problem is, we often fail to read the material.

Before we go into detail about the characteristics of the four styles, let's practice reading the behaviors. We have established the fact that you already know how to read the behavior because you were able to come up with an assertive person in your mind. Bring that person up in your conscious mind again. Picture him or her as he walks into a room. Remember, avoid the temptation to make judgments about what he is thinking or what his behavior means. Just look at the behavior and let's see if we can describe it with adjectives.

Picture that person coming into a room where you are an uninvolved observer. What is his behavior? How does he walk, talk, act. What is his body language, tone of voice, volume, etc. What facial expressions do you see? Before you read on, take a moment and jot down in the space below the adjectives you would use to describe this behavior:

The chances are your list of adjectives will look something like this:

Loud, willing to use volume when necessary
Initiating, they start the conversation, always have something going.
Fast
walking
talking
deciding
Lots of arm movement (it may be closed or open, depending on their emotional openness).
Strong eye contact, they look you right in the eye.
Leaning in, invading the other's personal space or privacy bubble. (The "privacy bubble" is that space that we all have that defines how close we stand to one another. If you invade my privacy bubble I get very uncomfortable. You can observe this discomfort on a crowded elevator where everyone's space is violated. We all back up to the wall and face the door, look at the numbers to avoid eye contact. If you want to test people's nervousness in this situation, get on a crowded elevator sometime and don't turn around. Just look them right in the eye. You will see a lot of squirming.)
A firm handshake.
Facial expression might be stern or expressive but it is not bland.

Now let's look at the opposite end of the spectrum, the ask assertive. The adjectives we choose might be the opposite of the tell assertive but, again, picture someone you know who is very ask assertive. See him in a room, at a party, at a business meeting, or whatever. What are his behaviors? Jot them down:

Very likely you came up with adjectives like:

Quiet, speaks when spoken to.
Not an initiator, waits for someone else to start the conversation or present an idea.
Slow
    walking
    talking
    deciding
Little arm movement or body language. His hands and arms seem to be close in to his body most of the time. What arm movement there is is slow, deliberate.
Little or no eye contact. He may look you in the eye for a moment while he listens to your question but then while he thinks of an answer he will look up at the ceiling or down at the floor.
Leans backward, avoiding invading other's privacy and protecting his own space. (You say, "Wait, if they lean backward they'll fall over." But watch ask assertive people in conversation; they may have their hand to their chin and their shoulders will actually be behind their feet. Now they will have one foot out in front to balance themselves but nonetheless they are leaning back.)
A less firm handshake. This guideline can be deceiving because some ask assertive people have trained themselves to shake hands firmly and have made a habit of it.
Facial expression is seldom exaggerated. It may be stern if he is at the top of the responsiveness axis but more than likely it will

merely be expressionless. At the bottom of the responsiveness axis it may be smiling but the smile will not be a big grin.

At this point let's begin to look at some of the advantages of knowing a person's style. We have said that the tell assertive person is fast, in walk, talk, and deciding. If we are trying to convince someone that our solution will indeed solve their problem we need to know their decision pattern. Once I was working with the president of a very profitable medium-sized bank who's style was tell assertive. I asked him how many decisions he might make in a day.

He said, "I don't know. Maybe a hundred or more." I asked, "How many of these would you expect to be correct?"

He said, "I feel like I'm ahead of the game if I get 51 percent right. The rest I change tomorrow."

I had another client who also was the president of a very profitable medium-sized bank who was off the chart on the ask assertive side. I asked him how many decisions he might make in a day. The question itself seem to create tension for him.

He said, "As few as absolutely possible. Maybe five or six."

I said, "How many of those do you expect to be correct?"

He stiffened and looked at me as though I had asked the ridiculous. "They'd better *all* be right," was his curt answer.

Now if you are trying to sell your solution to either of these people you need to know that their snap decisions or their hesitations may have little if anything to do with your proposal but much to do with their own style.

As an aside, notice that I have presented two people who have been equally successful in the same field. Yet they have attained that success with opposite styles. In all of my studies, and in other studies I have read, I have never found any correlation between success in dealing with people (management or sales) and the different Social Styles[SM]. There is, however, a great deal of correlation between success and one's versatility, which to a large extent measures the endorsement one receives from using his or her style behavior effectively with other people.

Now let's look at the responsiveness axis before going into detail on the third element of behavior, versatility.

Responsiveness measures the effort that a person makes to show or control his emotions or feelings publicly. Again, people will fall anywhere on a spectrum between the extremes but for the purposes of clarity let us look at just two people, one at the top of the axis, the *very* emotionally controlled person and the other at the bottom, the *very* emotionally open person.

Let's start with control. We all know someone who is a poker-faced, cool, aloof person. The very terms *cool* and *aloof* seem to turn us off. But if we think about it, if, say, our building is on fire, do we want someone to come running in, flailing his arms and yelling, "The place is on fire. We've gotta get out of here"? Or would we rather have a cool, aloof person come in deliberately and announce in a controlled voice that there is an emergency and then give us direct instructions for evacuating? The answer is obvious.

Let us list some of the adjectives we would use to describe the person at the very top of the responsiveness axis, that person who is the most controlled. List them here:

Your list might look something like this:

Cool
Aloof
Poker-faced
Hard to get to know
Not apparently friendly
Closed body language (if controlled people are assertive then we
    know the body language is out from the body but it is closed in
    the sense that the arms are not spread apart. They may be
    pointing their index finger or have both hands gesturing out
    in front of their body but close together. You can't get to them.
    If they are ask assertive then their arms will be close in,
    folded, or their hands will be clasped closed in front. They may

have one arm across their body with the other elbow resting on it and their fist to their chin.)

Task-oriented (talks about work, getting the job done, goals, objectives)

Fact-oriented (speaks of numbers, dollar amounts, specifics. If you ask him a people question he will answer in the number of people that do specific tasks.)

Untouchable (you know instinctively that you don't touch this person except in clearly defined rituals such as hand shaking)

Formal dress (doesn't loosen his tie unless it is a clearly defined "work-related situation"; the woman keeps her jacket on)

If your list looked about like this one then you are well on your way to reading this aspect of behavior. If you have a question about people who are closer to the center then listen to the words they use. Are they fact-filled with lots of numbers or do they talk about people and feelings. Facts and numbers place them above the midline; people and feeling words place them below.

Now make a list of the adjectives you would use to describe the person at the bottom of the responsiveness axis, that person that "lets it all hang out."

Perhaps your list looked about like this:

Warm

Friendly

Easy to get to know

Open body language (if he is assertive then that openness is outstretched arms—in a welcoming attitude if he is happy to see you—in an outstretched flailing of the fists if he is angry).

People-oriented

Feelings-oriented ("Joe makes you feel good, just being with

him." "I get choked up when I hear a story like that." "Gosh,
you're funny. I can hardly wait for your next witty remark.")

Touching (if he is tell assertive he will initiate hugs or will grab
your arm with his left hand when he shakes hands with his
right. If he is ask assertive he won't initiate touching. But, you
don't tell these people you are sorry to hear about their
problems without a hug or at least a pat on the shoulder.)

Informal dress (more apt to wear a sports coat or sporty attire,
will loosen his tie or remove his jacket)

If your list looked something like this one then you know how to
read the emotionally open person.

As we have stated, most of us fall somewhere in between the
extremes. If you are trying to place someone on the responsiveness
axis who is nearer the middle, place check marks by the adjectives
that describe that person. If you have more check marks below the
line than above you probably have an emotionally open person.
Similarly, if you have more check marks above the line then that
person is probably less emotionally outgoing.

Now let's look again at the four quadrants:

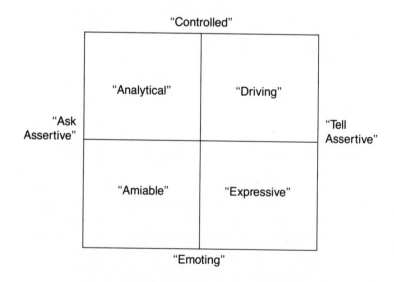

The Social Style^{SM} Model used by permission.

In my experience I have learned to look for other clues that might indicate what quadrant a person falls into.

I have noticed that many people with the driving style will have an austere office with a clean desk. They have delegated everything that comes to their desk or they have taken care of it and dispatched it. Remember they make fast decisions and move on.

They ask pointed questions to aid them in their quick decisions, which are made on general facts, not details.

The expressive style often has a cluttered desk. I have been in many of their offices where there are plaques and pictures honoring the incumbent of the office. Every award they have ever gotten is proudly displayed on their walls—even those from grade school. They may have pictures of the family but the expressive is right in the middle of the picture. "Here *I* am, showing off *my* family."

The amiable style is relationship-oriented. Their relationship skills show in their work. They will likely have a small personal plant (not just one owned by the plant-leasing company). They are family-oriented so there will be pictures of the family, often without them in the picture.

In my experience, the analyticals tend to put plaques or awards on the wall only from institutions or persons for whom they have high regard, accomplishments of which they are very proud.

Now let's look at some specific attributes of each of the four Social Style℠ positions that will give us guidelines for how to deal with each one.

The Driving Style

Is a control specialist. They take charge of every situation. When I divide people into small groups in my seminars they will ask, "Is the driver the one who becomes the group leader?" I say, "No, he or she is the one who 'appoints' the leader. 'You'll make a good leader. You do it.'"

The theme that runs through their lives is that of action. If you work for them and there is a crisis, don't sit and try to think what to do. They will say, "Think on your own time. Get on the phone and make something happen."

Is motivated by measurable results. We all want results but for these people to feel successful the results must be measurable. They can count it in dollars or weigh it or in some way measure the results objectively.

Fears being taken advantage of. Their motivation answers their fear. If they can objectively measure their results then they know they have not been taken advantage of.

The Expressive Style

Is people-oriented. They see the world as basically friendly but feel that people must be "sold" on their ideas. People have to be motivated, inspired to follow their direction.

The theme that runs through their lives is intuition. They will make fast decisions but they will be made on "gut feel." "You're my kind of people," they will say. "I think we can work together."

Is motivated by applause. People in the lower right extreme cannot get enough praise.

Fears loss of social approval. If they are in a room with 100 people, 99 of whom love them and one of whom doesn't like them, they will be talking to that one trying to convince them that they are lovable. If they are getting applause or praise then they know they are approved of.

The Amiable Style

Is a support specialist. They remember your birthday, ask about your sick relative, send flowers on appropriate occasions.

The theme that runs through their lives is that of relationship. They are constantly aware of their relationships with those around them. The relationship amiables have with you when they first meet you is important enough that they do not want to hurt your feelings. The truth is less important than making you happy. They tend to tell you what they think you want to hear.

They are motivated by safety, the safety of the status quo. They are very reluctant to make changes. They are very good at following rules and procedures. They make decisions only when they have guidelines that fit the situation, which will dictate how the decision is to be made.

They fear change. These people are very disturbed by changes in personnel, bosses, etc. They don't tend to change jobs often and have problems handling being let go. They don't even like to change the office they occupy.

The Analytical Style

Is a technical specialist. They handle detail work well. They may
not like it but they handle it well. They tend to make checklists
to see that all the procedures are followed. They are impressed
only with institutions, people, and processes for which they
have high regard.

The theme that runs through their lives is that of thinking. You
ask them what time it is and they tell you how the watch is
made. They want to explain how they arrived at a conclusion.
The process is almost more important than the result. They
want to know about your process in solving their problem.

You motivate them by assuring them that they are right. There
must be guarantees. Acceptance of your proposal is strongly
dependent on proof that it is the right process. They will be
influenced by recommendations of others only if those others
are held in high regard by the analytical.

They fear criticism of their work. They are very sensitive to errors
in their process and may try to convince you that they are right
and that your criticism is invalid.

Please keep in mind that you cannot put people in boxes. No
one's characteristics fall 100 percent into one style. However, most
people have a home base that will have a number of the tendencies
of one style. If we keep this in mind, then the guidelines will be of a
good bit of value.

Each of the four styles has its own decision-making process.

Being tell assertive, the driving style makes fast decisions. His
decisions are based on fact or tasks. He tends to skip over details
and make decisions based on broad facts. Often he will have
another person working with him that is detail-oriented. If he
respects that person he may rely on that person's opinion of the
details.

He will asked direct, even rude questions to gain enough
information for his decision. Once I presented a proposal to an
analytical who worked for a driver. My analytical called his driver-
boss to tell him I was there with the proposal. My analytical, of
course, had thoroughly studied the proposal down to the last detail.

The driver-boss came into the office, looked at all the headings
as he flipped through the proposal, looked at the price, then asked

the analytical, "Are you satisfied with the details?" The answer was "Yes."

Then he looked at me and said, "Are you worth this much money?" The abruptness of the question almost threw me, but I realized I had a driver on my hands and blurted out a firm, "Yes."

"Let's hire him." And he left the office as fast as he had entered.

The expressive also makes fast decisions but these tend to be made based on a "gut feel" rather than facts. The sales process with an expressive may be less structured than with the others. It's hard to get him to sit down and follow a proposal through from start to finish. He will look at headings but he'd really rather talk about it. I had one of these fellows put my proposal aside after a cursory look. Then he looked at me, smiled, and said, "Dick, why don't you tell me what's in that proposal."

It's not that these people are necessarily too lazy to read; it's just that they gather their information from people and that is part of their decision-making process.

By the way, I didn't really expect my expressive to listen to what I had to say about the proposal. I started the discussion knowing I would be interrupted. And I was, several times.

The amiable's decision-making style is much more labored. When selling to these people it is wise not to push. Patience is a virtue here. Often amiables need assurances from people with whom they have close relationships. Amiables often are put in positions to make the decision the boss would make. They are most comfortable when a decision can be made according to well-structured guidelines.

If he is the boss then recommendations from his close friends are helpful. "Your good friend Ruth Davis has been using our service for years. You might want to visit with her about how she feels about us." Then give him plenty of time to check with Ruth.

The analytical is also slow to decide. He or she must study the proposal. He will mentally "try out" the answers that you have proposed. He may want a test case. He will want options to change the direction in midstream if it isn't working. Strong guarantees are important to him.

Recommendations from others can be useful if the analytical holds the other person in high esteem. Just because his competitor uses your service may not mean a thing to our analytical. He may feel his competitor is a jerk and unable to make good decisions.

Most of all the nonassertive people need time. His delays may drive you crazy but his style calls for caution.

Now let's assume you have read your prospect's behavioral style and you have him or her fairly well fixed in one of the four quadrants. Now what do you do? How do you deal with that person to facilitate a better relationship?

The answer is, "Versatility." That is the third aspect of behavior that we read in others. We spot others' willingness to adjust their behavior in order to accommodate us. Others will spot that ability in us. Used in moderation it is a very effective tool in building and maintaining relationships in both business and in our personal lives.

The next chapter will define versatility in terms of each of the four styles and give examples for its importance in dealing with each style.

7

We Spoke Spanish

I walked through the door of the bank's marketing department and Carol was the first person I saw. Carol had a wild mane of reddish-blonde hair. She was attractive, animated, extroverted.

With outstretched arms she almost yelled, "Dick Kendall. Here's the man who's going to tell us how to market this bank." With a grand gesture to her secretary she exclaimed, "This man is the country's foremost expert on bank marketing." Her arms were extended to me as though I were being introduced for an award. She was smiling all this time. She was bigger than life. I was almost embarrassed by how she welcomed me.

There is no doubt I had an expressive on my hands. Carol was a classic, in the lower right-hand corner of the model. I was totally taken in. I teach this stuff, but I didn't suspect a thing. However, Carol was feeling threatened. The boss (an analytical, by the way) had brought in an "expert" to "help" Carol do a better job.

Here's the situation. Another banker had recommended me to Carol's boss. The bank was in a medium-sized city in West Texas. The boss, Bill, told me on the phone, "I don't know what Carol is doing. She's plenty bright. She's got a great background in real estate marketing. I think she just doesn't understand the banking world."

I suggested I come write a marketing plan for the bank. "Yeah. A plan. That's what she needs." Analyticals love plans. Expressives, by the way, do not.

Perhaps I didn't mention that I fall somewhere near the middle of the style model in the analytical quadrant. I understood Bill and his need for a plan. He had a bank to run. He needed to be right. I could do that for him.

Carol swooped me into her office and began telling me what a wonderful job she was doing in the two weeks she had been with the bank. "This bank needs me and I'm going to turn it around." Expressives are not shy about tooting their own horn.

Then she gave me a tour of the bank. As we walked through the bank and met people she told me stories about everyone and how they were helping with the marketing programs. She told me about training programs she had started. She told me about seeing the long lines at the drive-in on the first Friday afternoon she was here. The next week she had organized a task force from among the employees to serve lemonade and smiles to those waiting in the long line.

"The customers *loved* it. The employees loved it. They all love me, too." She actually said that.

I was witnessing Carol's "backup styles." This is where you go when you are threatened, under pressure, your relationship tension is high. In backup style everyone goes to their corner. In my case, as an analytical I became less assertive and more aloof. I begin to think about leaving. "When will five o'clock get here?" When does my plane leave?" If leaving is not an option I get very quiet, get a sober expression on my face, ask a few questions and say "hmmm" a lot.

Expressives, on the other hand, go to their corner. They get more tell assertive and more open and personal. Since they need applause, they brag on themselves if no one else will. They get more animated, more personal, more in your face. In a word, Carol. Carol threatened me and I started reacting in my typical analytical backup fashion.

Now, interestingly, while Carol's backup style was threatening me, what do you think my backup style was doing to her? My sober expression and saying "hmmm" was driving her up the wall. She was not getting through to me so she had to work harder at it. More animation, more stories, more bragging. Of course, I responded with more sober looks, more silence, more "hmmm's." We were on a collision course.

Finally, after the tour, she parked me in her office and excused herself for some important business. At last I was left alone. Peace and quiet. I looked at my watch. I looked at the airline tickets. It was 11:00 A.M. The plane didn't leave until 5:00. Six more hours with this monster.

Then a small opening came in my mind and a ray of light shone in. "Dick, you teach this stuff. How could you be so unaware of what is going on? You've got a style problem.

"Let's see. What is Carol's style? Expressive, of course. What does she need? Applause. What good can I say about this woman?" Then everything inside of me began to shout, "Nothing. Nothing. There is no redeeming value whatsoever in this bragging, self-aggrandizing, overdramatic broad."

Then reason set in. Once I began to think about her instead of me, my relationship tension began to drop. My feeling of avoidance began to subside and I could think more clearly. Analyticals think quite well when we are on the task-tension side of the defensiveness model.

She needed applause. I needed to brag on her. I began to replay our first hour together. She had been at the bank a few weeks. In our tour she had introduced me to every employee by name, first and last. She called their children by name in the stories she told. She bragged on each one, giving specific examples of how they had helped with the lemonade or participated in the training.

People's faces had lit up when Carol came into the room. She was the most exciting thing to hit the bank since the new computer was installed. I'm the one who says you market a bank with people. And here was a people specialist doing her people thing at its best. There was a lot about Carol to brag about.

It was time to adapt my style. Carol came back into the office. She sat down behind her desk. I got up on the edge of my chair and leaned into her across the desk. With some animation and excitement in my voice I said, "Carol! You're doing a great job in this bank. I'm really impressed. You called everybody we talked to today by name. Do you know the names of every employee in this bank? There must be a hundred or more." I used more inflections than I might normally. I was a little louder than my norm. I even waved my hands and arms a little as I made these points.

I could almost see Carol's tension lessen. Her ruffled feathers began to smooth out. She sat back in her chair, she sighed, and in a much less frantic tone she said, "Yeah. I think learning people's names is important. So I've worked hard at it. I think I've about got 'em all."

"And tell me some more about the training program. I can tell these people are responding to what you are trying to teach them. They all seem to like you."

We were off and running. I didn't have to keep up the bragging and arm waving all day. A little goes a long way. I did show a little emotion when I told her boss how impressed I was with her, but I was still so much lower key than Carol that Bill didn't seem to notice.

That afternoon as I was leaving to catch my plane she walked me out to my car. As I unlocked the door she took my arm and said, "Dick, can I level with you?"

I said, "Sure."

"This morning after I gave you the tour I left you in my office and I went out and all but screamed at my secretary. I said, 'What a stuffed shirt this guy is. I'll never be able to work with him.' But, Dick, now that I've gotten to know you I couldn't have been more wrong. We're going to do great things for this bank together. I can hardly wait for you to come back and get us started."

A lot of my analytical friends tell me that I was being phony with Carol. Granted, I felt uncomfortable when I was being animated about her great people skills. The animation is uncomfortable for me because it's not my style. That doesn't make it wrong or phony. What I was doing was adapting my style, being uncomfortable, so that she could be comfortable. Put another way, I quit insisting that we speak only my language and began speaking hers. That's called versatility.

In the middle fifties, when I was in college, I went to school in Mexico for a summer. I lived with a group of Mexican college students. We got to be great friends. We went to class and movies together. I was even invited along to serenade a girlfriend. They still did that then. We had a band with us. She came out on the balcony. He threw her a rose. There was a beautiful moon. Romantic.

The thing I remember about Mexico is that I spoke Spanish. It was fun but it was difficult. Now I could have gone to Mexico with the attitude that English was my native language and it would be phony for me to speak Spanish. I would be pretending I was something I wasn't, in this case a Mexican. I could have had that attitude but I would not have built any relationships with the Mexican people. As it was, I was willing to make myself uncomfortable in order to make others more comfortable and in order to build relationships.

I will feel uncomfortable for a time when I am speaking another language. I always feel uncomfortable speaking Spanish. What if I do it wrong? What if they expect me to know more of the language than I do? What if they use a word I don't know? What if I say *embarrasado* When I feel embarrassed? Look's right, doesn't it? *"Estoy embarrasado"* is Spanish for, "I am pregnant." That's an embarrassing mistake.

I'm uncomfortable speaking Spanish. I'm uncomfortable speaking expressive or driver or amiable. But you may be more comfortable and I'm willing to make that sacrifice temporarily if it will help us build a relationship. And, I should note, that the more I speak Spanish or expressive or driving or amiable, the more comfortable I get with it.

I have another client who is a driving style. He looks you right in the eye, asks pointed questions, needs direct confrontation. When I prepare for a meeting with him I get my facts together and I am ready for any question he might ask. I sit up a little toward the front of my seat and look him right in the eye. This is his behavior. By my matching his behavior to some extent we have a better relationship.

Years ago when I was first introduced to the concept of styles I was very defensive about being told that I was an analytical. Before I got my feedback an instructor was going through the four styles. I decided that the place to be was a near-center expressive, assertive but not pushy, friendly and open but not gushy. What a surprise when my feedback showed me that I was a near-center analytical, aloof but not cold, ask assertive but not a wallflower. I was offended. It hurt my feelings. I rejected the concept for a time. I decided that the feedback instrument was in error.

However, the idea kept rumbling around in my analytical mind. One day I had the unpleasant task of expressing my sympathy to a friend whose fourteen-year-old son had died. My friend is an amiable.

In my rather cool and aloof analytical fashion I said, "Gee, Don,

I'm really sorry." Suddenly I saw myself from the outside. I was cool, standing erect and expressionless. I found myself shaking hands in a very dispassionate manner as if I had just met Don. I could see that Don was a little put off. Out of nowhere some adaptability set in. Though very uncharacteristic of me, I found myself putting my left hand on Don't shoulder. Then, as if that weren't enough, I leaned over and hugged him. Don cried. I cried. We had connected.

I have thought about that moment many times since. It was at that moment that I accepted my style. By the same token I also realized that my style was not always sufficient to express my feelings. My feelings for Don were very real. I felt his hurt though I could only begin to imagine its depth. It was then that I realized that my style needed to be more adaptable. Hugging men is not part of my style, so in this case I had to "borrow" from Don's style. It worked. I was not phony in the least. I was merely using another style to express my true feelings in a way that Don could understand.

Versatility, according to the TRACOM model, is a measure of endorsement. In other words, the degree of acceptance accorded one by persons of various styles. In order to gain that endorsement we must adapt our behavior. How do we measure that endorsement? The TRACOM system, of course, is an excellent way. Other than that we can ask for feedback. Ask others how they see you, how they feel about you and your behavior. Our versatility *is* a major factor in our effectiveness in dealing with people, be it in sales or management.

Adapting my behavior is hard work. It is uncomfortable. I'm willing to be uncomfortable in order to make you comfortable. I don't have to adapt my behavior much in order to gain a greater endorsement from others. Most people find my thoughtful concentration reassuring. My attention to detail often gives others the feeling that things will be taken care of. It is only in critical moments, the first meeting, a decision time, a crisis, that some adaptation is needed.

As I have studied this concept (we analyticals always have to study things) I have come to realize that I have always known about adapting my behavior to meet the needs of various styles. An example is my relationship with my children. I have one daughter who is an analytical, like me, and another, younger daughter who is an expressive with amiable tendencies. I have always treated them differently.

Once when my analytical daughter was in high school we got a letter from the principal saying, "Congratulations on Peggy's acceptance into the Honor Society. I'm sorry you were unable to attend the installation ceremony."

I said, "Peggy. What's this?"

She shrugged and said, "Oh, it's nothing."

One of the reasons I'm writing this book is to brag on my kids. Peggy was in ninth place in a class of 900. Lots of kids made the Honor Society. Remember analyticals only put a plaque on the wall if they have a very high regard for the organization that awarded it. No organization that has lots of members is worthy of that esteem.

That night when I went into Peg's room to say good night, I sat on the edge of the bed and very quietly said, "Peg, your mother and I are really proud of how well you do in school. It makes me feel good to know you're in the Honor Society even though I know you take something like that for granted."

A tiny smile came into the corners of her mouth. "Thank you, Daddy." That was it. We had connected. Anything more would have been suspect. This was easy. It was analytical to analytical. No problem.

Susan was a different matter. I had to work a little at relating to her. She was smart in high school, too, but not quite as much a book learner as Peg, maybe the top 10 percent. Her thing was drama, acting, speech.

One time Susan won first place in a speech contest in another city. Do you think we had to wait for a letter from the principal? Ha. She phoned us the minute she found out. Although I think we could almost have heard her without the phone.

She arrived at the house late that afternoon. The front door flew open and in flew Susan. Now did I wait until bedtime to quietly tell her I was proud? "No way, José!"—her words, not mine.

I greeted her at the door and gave her a big hug. Then we held hands and bounced around the living room yelling, "We won. We won." And I hoped the neighbors weren't watching.

By the way, Peggy would often watch these episodes with some satisfaction, knowing that her little sister was getting what she needed. She also knew that Daddy would settle down to his analytical self whenever it was her turn.

Giving other people what they need in our relationships is not always acting the same way they do. We have people in our world because they like and need us the way we are. Many times my analytical style can be very calming and reassuring for the more tell assertive people. However, occasionally, I need to borrow from other people's styles to effect a better working relationship.

Once I had a secretary who was a classic amiable. She was a hard worker and really wanted to please me. But for some reason she never did anything right. A colleague of mine who is a very style-aware person suggested that my secretary might need good clear directions. Amiables like to know the rules and what is expected of them.

So that afternoon I went out to her desk and gave her some work, a report that needed to be cleaned up and retyped. Remembering my friend's suggestion I put on my driving hat and leaned in and gave her specific directions on how I wanted the report to look. Then I asked her to have it on my desk for my review at 3:30. She said, "Thank you."

I went in my office and closed the door and had terrible feelings of remorse. I had really hurt her feelings. I was too pushy. She would think I was mean. I actually had a stomach ache.

At 3:30 sharp she came into my office with the report done exactly the way I wanted it. As she walked out she stopped and turned around and said, "By the way, Dick, I really appreciate the clear instructions you gave me on this project. I knew exactly what you wanted and it really helped." I never stop learning.

Now let's relate this information to the sales call situation. People often come up to me at breaks during a seminar and ask, "What's my style." I usually don't know even though I may have been working with that person for several hours. Determining another's style takes effort. I'm usually too lazy to do it unless I have good reason. A sales call on an individual I don't know is good reason.

So one of the times I use my style-awareness skill is in a first call. I immediately look around the office for clues. Are there lots of plaques, pictures, awards? Is the desk clean or messy? These are not always indicators but I have found they give me an idea. I watch the behavior of the office incumbent. How do they greet me? What is the person's body language? What words do they use? Are they fact-and-task or people-and-feeling–oriented? I try to get a feel for style. If it is much different from mine then my first response is to slip into their style. I become more animated and talk faster if the incumbent is an expressive. I get right down to business if he's a driver. If he's an amiable I take time to talk about feelings, weather, pretty things in the office. I try to find mutual acquaintances. If he is an analytical I look for connections with college diplomas. I comment on the plaques that are on the wall because these are important. I talk about processes. I compliment clearly well-done work.

These little changes in my behavior and the recognition of the needs of the person on whom I'm calling go a long way toward opening a working relationship.

Though I'm aware of the style differences, if they exist I don't have to think much about them until there is a critical change or a presentation of a proposal in which I'm asking for change. At that point I always take into account the style of the person to whom I am presenting the proposal. If the proposal is a written proposal and I have time to think about it in the privacy of my office, I picture the person who will receive it. What is his style? I then slant the wording and style of the proposal to match.

I also try to determine who else will be seeing the proposal. Are there other styles involved? One approach is to write the proposal in outline format. The major headings will satisfy the driving or expressive style person while the smaller headings will provide detail for the analytical. Amiables will look over the list of references. In a later chapter we will talk about what I call a background summary, which I usually include at the beginning of a proposal. This is a summary of my understanding of the client's situation, problems, and needs. This part of the proposal is often written to reflect the style of the recipient. If the person has a driving style then the summary is curt and to the point, just enough to show that I have a grasp of the problems. For an expressive, a little bragging about the client's successes is in order. For the amiable a recognition of the relationships within the firm and between the firm and its customers is appropriate. For the analytical correct detail with an emphasis on process is important. By the way, I always ask the client to read over the summary to make sure I have not made any mistakes. The analytical will accept the thoroughness of this approach even though there are needed corrections.

The presentation of the proposal is also critical. The driving style needs a few highlights sufficient to make a decision. The expressive style appreciates fanfare, pomp and circumstance. The amiable style likes to have others in the meeting to support the final decision. The analytical is interested in the details of the process that will be used in effecting the proposed solution.

The decision style of each is also important. The analytical and amiable are probably not going to make snap decisions on important issues. They need time: the analytical to study the proposal, the amiable to share and discuss it with others. Pushing these two is a mistake.

During the presentation the person with a driving style will expect quick answers to questions. I try to study all possible questions before I go to a meeting in which I will be presenting to a driver. I have the answers on the tip of my tongue.

The expressive will want time to talk and will expect compliments on things already done. Show-and-tell works better here than the quiet reading of the proposal. Pictures, descriptions, and story telling are all more acceptable. Involvement on the part of the expressive is good if it fits into the presentation.

The amiable will need time to review the proposal with others. Examples of how people in other organizations reacted to the proposed work are helpful. Relationships are important and your examples should show how these will be strengthened by the proposed work.

The analytical will want detail. Assurances of success are also critical. Guarantees that allow a back door for the analytical are also very helpful. Proof of success in other situations is important. The analytical is very apt to check out the veracity of your story, by the way. Your facts need to be exact.

Another time for the awareness of styles is when conflict arises. This can be true when you are trying to motivate an employee as well as trying to sell a client or prospect.

For instance we always hear that we need to use praise in dealing with employees. This is true to some extent. But style is important when using praise as a motivator. A classic expressive can't get enough praise. You can say, "Wow, Barbara, that report was outstanding. You had 'em cheering in the bleachers." The response will be an inflation, a desire to do more. You can say it again the next day and see them puff up again, and maybe even next week.

But if you try that on the driving style your response may be something like, "Yeah. I told you I was good at that." Then the next time you praise the driver you may get a curt, "Hey, if I'm so good how about a raise." You see, they need measurable results.

The second time you praise an analytical he quietly wonders what you are trying to sell. The amiable will spend so much time telling you who else deserves the credit for the success that you won't waste time praising him again.

Versatility, the endorsement of your behavior, is the key to success in relationships, whether you are selling to people or managing them or just trying to have a meaningful relationship with them.

Now to answer a few questions about style. At this point some people say, "I don't have a particular style. I move all over the chart to suit the situation."

That may be true, but it probably isn't. Get some feedback from people who know you well. Let them read the last two chapters and get them to tell you about your behaviors. Most of us have a home base and we tend to stay pretty close to it. When we do move out of our comfort range the change is often so dramatic that we feel like we have moved much further than we really have.

I have taught this concept in a two-day seminar format for the University of Kentucky Engineering School's continuing-education program. These courses are attended by alumnae from all over the state. At the end of the day I hand out the feedback instruments that show each participant what his style is. Then I tell the class to practice "what they are not." In other words, I tell them to try some tell assertive behavior if their style is ask assertive and vice versa.

At one class I started day two by asking the participants if any of them had practiced their opposite behavior. One hand timidly went up. I asked that person what he did.

In a quiet voice he said, "I sent my steak back at the restaurant last night. I was really assertive." At that there were snickers from four or five of the other participants. I asked one of the others to describe what had happened.

The group had eaten together at the hotel restaurant. "You

should have seen him. He first sat there looking at his steak. Finally, he looked up and caught the waiter's eye. The waiter immediately came over and asked if something was wrong. He said, 'Gosh, this is really a fine restaurant and your service has been wonderful. And...and, I really hate to complain but...well, you see, I...I...really like my steak a little more done.' The waiter took the steak and assured him that it was no problem."

That person confided that he had never sent a meal back in his life. He had moved a little to the right on the assertive scale and since it was so foreign to him he felt as though he had gone off the chart on the assertive side. Get some feedback on your actual behavior and you will probably find that you tend to stay close to your home base most of the time.

The next question that I often hear is, "Where is the best place to be on the Social Style Model?" The answer is, "Where you are." This is home base for you. You have spent a lifetime developing that style. It works for you. Use it to its best advantage. In all of the studies of style that I have seen there is no correlation between style and success in work or play. This is equally true for people in sales as well as for managers and even presidents of huge corporations.

In my seminars I will have participants place U.S. presidents on the Social Style Model. We always get Nixon in the upper right driving position, Lyndon Johnson falls in the expressive quadrant, Eisenhower the amiable corner, and Lincoln the analytical. I use these examples because, no matter what you may have thought of the politics of the presidents mentioned, you will have to admit that they were successful. They all reached the highest office in our land. You may have disagreed with what they did once they got there but being president of the United States has to be considered a success.

I used to use four whodunit heroes in the same manner. Kojak, Barreta, Columbo, and Barnaby Jones each fit within different quadrants of the style model. Yet each one "got his man." They were successful using their own unique style.

Another aspect of style awareness that should be noted is what is known as "backup style." This is the way people behave when their back is to the wall, under pressure. We all tend to "go to our corner" whenever our relationship tension is high.

The person with a driving style becomes more assertive and more controlled and becomes dictatorial. He or she starts barking orders and tries to take charge, to get things moving, to solve the problem.

The expressive becomes more assertive and more emoting. He or she attacks the source of the problem, be it a person, an institution, or a thing.

The amiable becomes still less assertive and more emoting. They acquiesce. They give in. They tell you what they think you want to hear. "OK. You're right. We'll do it your way." A week later, of course, they continue to do it their way. They pay you compliments (which drives the driving style crazy) and tell you how much they think of you. Sometimes they cry.

The analytical becomes less assertive and more controlled. They do everything possible to avoid the situation. I got into a heated argument with a fellow worker once in the office of a classic analytical. In a few minutes we looked up and saw he was gone. He had left his own office to avoid the conflict. True to my analytical style I have devised a thousand ways of avoiding threatening situations. I ask for more time to study the problem. I go to check the files. I call a meeting. The purpose is to avoid the conflict or situation that is causing the relationship tension.

Knowing style, being aware that others' styles are unique and have value, and learning to be more adaptable in dealing with other styles will all go a long way toward success in selling your solutions for others' problems. It also can be very helpful in dealing with your fellow workers, your subordinates, your bosses, and even your family and friends. No one gets it right 100 percent of the time. We analyticals want to be right 100 percent of the time. But practice does make perfect, or at least it goes a long way in building good, strong relationships.

8

Winning Friends and Influencing People

"The important thing is not to stop questioning. Curiosity has its own reason for existing. One cannot help but be in awe when he contemplates the mysteries of eternity, of life, of the marvelous structure of reality. It is enough if one tries merely to comprehend a little of this mystery everyday. Never lose a holy curiosity."

—ALBERT EINSTEIN

I once asked a very successful salesperson, "What is your greatest asset when it comes to selling." His simple reply: "My ears."

Listening is the key to understanding. Understanding is the basis of all relationships.

We have set up the call we are making with a Call Purpose Statement. The Call Purpose Statement has established a reason for us to learn about the clients' business, goals, and problems. I usually end my Call Purpose Statement with something like, "So it would really help me if you just told me a little about your business." This can be tailored to your call purpose. It might be something like, "Tell me about your department... section ...job...goals, etc.

In many cases that is enough to get the prospect off and running. Other times I have to add a question to help get him started. He might say, "Well, what do you want to know?"

Now comes the questioning part. An integral part of listening is asking good questions. Early on in the conversation I want to ask open-ended questions that allow ample room for the prospect to show me what is important to him.

At the opening of the conversation I can take three tracks, whichever seems appropriate. I may say, "How did you get started in this business?" This is the historic approach. The other two involve process and market. The process question might be, "What do you do?" The market approach might be, "Who do you do this for?" I have never failed to get a good, lengthy response to one of these questions.

Once I was making a sales call on behalf of a bank. The name of the company on which I was calling was rather generic. It did not describe the business. The business was located in an old automobile dealership. The back shop was used for manufacturing. The owner's office was one of the little offices off the showroom. As I entered I almost stumbled over hundreds of oddshaped metal pieces, the likes of which I had never seen before. They were laid out in rows, each with its own tag.

So when the question "What do you want to know about my business?" came, my next question was obvious.

"What *is* all that stuff out there," I said.

He laughed.

"That's what we do," he said. "Come on, I'll show you." He took me out to explain the parts. The natural next step was a tour of the back shop, the manufacturing facility. It turned out that they manufactured small parts for some kind of offshore-drilling equipment.

By the time we returned to the owner's office I had a thorough understanding of his business and a head full of questions about people, financial relationships, goals, problems, and soon. We talked for over an hour. He had problems. My bank had solutions. We got his business.

If I'm talking to the owner the historical approach is usually best. "How did you get in this business?" Most people are proud of the business they have. If I present myself as a professional, trustworthy, they usually welcome an opportunity to brag about what they have done.

A variation of this question for nonowners might be "How did you come to be associated with _____? or "Tell me about your background in the _____ business."

The market approach asks about customers. "Who do you do this for?" It might come after you have information on the history and products. Or it might be an alternative when you know the history and products of a prospect and the person on whom you are calling knows you do.

By the way, I never assume that my prospect knows what I know. Even when I'm calling on a good customer I review with the customer what I know and what I have in my records.

That conversation might start with, "John, in preparing for my visit with you today I checked over my files and read my notes from my last call. Let me summarize what I found and make sure I've got an accurate record."

In the case of the prospect where it would be logical for me to do some research ahead, I would still review what I know. I might say something like, "The XYZ directory shows that you manufacture widgets, have been in business since 1945, and that you are family-owned. Is that information accurate? I never totally trust the directories."

Part of the purpose of reviewing previously acquired information is to bring the client or prospect along with your thinking. It shows understanding and brings this information to the forefront of the prospect's mind. And it connects this call with the last one. In addition, the review shows that you heard the prospect the last time and have some understanding of his business.

We'll add some other questions later. But first let's talk about listening. Most of us think of ourselves as good listeners. Most of us aren't. Listening is a skill. It has to be learned and practiced. It takes a conscious effort. If you think you are always a good listener, ask yourself about the last time you met a stranger. Did you remember his name? Often I meet someone, engage in some conversation, and then think, "What is this guy's name?" I haven't listened.

One of the problems with listening is the speed at which most people talk, which is about 150 to 200 words per minute. Research has shown that our brains can absorb about 500 words per minute.

So we have a 300- to 350-word excess capacity. It is what we do with the at excess capacity that determines our ability to listen.

One of the most common faults in listening is that we use that excess capacity for things other than focusing on the prospect and what he is saying.

One trick for using the excess capacity is to review what has just been said. Did we understand it? Did it fit within the context of our understanding of the business? Are there other questions we should ask to clarify what has been said? If so, what are those questions?

Another trick is to anticipate what is about to be said. If the prospect says, "Well, our profit margin is pretty good," we can put a percentage figure on the margin. "I bet he will say the profit margin is 25 percent," we might think. Then when he gives us a figure we can determine if we were right, and reinforce our memory of that figure, or if we were wrong, in which case we can consider why we were off. Or we might formulate some questions about why the figure is so high or so low.

Which brings up another trick for using the excess capacity: comparing this prospect's business with other businesses with which we are familiar. A statement such as, "In my dealings with other businesses similar to yours, the profit margin on X part of the business is usually higher. Is that true with your business?" This shows the prospect some of your familiarity with his business and at the same time shows that you are willing to see his business as unique.

Another aspect of listening is taking notes. I almost always take notes when interviewing a prospect. There are several good reasons for this. The first, of course, is that it enhances my memory of what I have heard. When writing a Summary Feedback (see chapter 9), I am always thankful for full notes. It makes the job so much simpler and doesn't tax my memory.

Another reason is that is shows the prospect you are serious about learning about his business. Let's say you come to my office, trying to get my banking business, and offer a good Call Purpose Statement that shows you want to learn about my business. Then you fail to take notes. I might well question your sincerity. I may have some fear that you will confuse what I tell you with what the next prospect tells you, particularly if I know you are making other calls.

Taking notes on a legal pad also gives you a certain authority. It is as if you were a lawyer preparing for a case. It gives more formality to the interview.

I always ask permission to take notes, however. After my Call Purpose Statement and my first question, I wait for the first answers to come. When I hear some information I want to remember I reach for my briefcase, take out a legal pad, and say, "By the way, do you mind if I take notes." You are dealing with the prospect's confidential information. He has a right to refuse your note taking. He probably never will, by the way. I have never had anyone refuse. They are usually flattered that I am so serious about their business.

Occasionally I will have a prospect who will talk about a new product or service or who for some other reason feels that what he is about to reveal is very confidential. He will sometimes say something about not wanting this to get out to the competition. In that case I will rather ceremoniously put down my pen and say, "I won't even put it in my notes, then." I seldom forget that kind of information anyway.

Note taking is also a way of reinforcing the listening. Taking a note tells the prospect that you think what he has just said is important. It may even cause the prospect to expand on that particular subject. Sometimes I may say something like "Really?," gesturing with my pen and then purposely focusing on that particular note.

If there is a rather lengthy or complex item I may even say "Wait, wait, I want to make sure I get this," and take a moment to write out the details. I may even read it back to the prospect to make sure I have it correct. "You mean that you have actually gotten your suppliers to warehouse their parts on your location in order to give you just-in-time delivery? That's pretty impressive."

Your notes will not be complete. Mine seldom are. I'll write one or two words of a thought and then be caught up in the questioning and listening. On my best days I go over my notes as soon as I get to the car and try to fill in the blanks while my memory is fresh. I recommend that highly. I personally either forget it or am in too much of a hurry to take time to do it. At any rate, if I write up my notes fairly soon after the call I can usually make some sense of the scratches.

In his book *Swim With the Sharks Without Being Eaten Alive*, Harvey Mackay titles one of his chapters on selling "Knowing Something About Your Customer Is Just as Important as Knowing Everything About Your Product." He then presents a sixty-six-question customer profile, which his sales people have to fill out on every customer.

Now let's expand on the questioning process. Here are a few tricks that help me in keeping the conversation going. By the way, please note that these tricks are worked on me, not the prospect. I still don't believe in tricking someone else.

We have already asked some open-ended questions to get the conversation started. The answers to the first questions will give us ideas about other questions we can ask. Early on we want to keep the questions open-ended. We are looking for the prospect's history, goals, and problems. Leaving the conversation open and free-flowing will give him the freedom to show us the direction of his concerns.

When we see that direction begin to take shape, then we can get more specific. One of the tricks I use in helping me to stay focused is to pretend that I have to show someone else through the business right after I get through with the interview. This helps me phrase the questions that I might be asked if I really did give such a tour. That happened to me once, as a matter of fact. I went off on a preliminary trip to sell a business on moving its manufacturing facility to our town, where I was the chamber of commerce manager. Later, I took some of our board members to that plant. I really did end up giving the tour.

The owner made the comment "This fellow knows more about this business than I do." It impressed my board members. I confess, it impressed me. That has never happened again but I keep thinking that it might and I want to be ready. It has helped in my questioning and listening.

Another trick is what I call my B.I.F. model. I it is an acronym, obviously. (No book that doesn't introduce at least one acronym into our culture will be a success.) Anyway, B.I.F. stands for the way most business are organized. They have a Back door, through which goods or raw materials are brought, and Inside, where a process takes place, and a Front door, through which sales are made. The model might look like this:

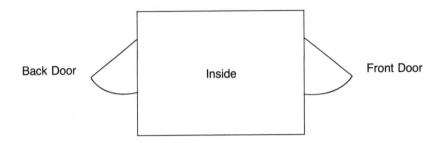

Back Door   Inside   Front Door

The back door has to do with purchases, suppliers, accounts payable, incoming shipping, all the things that a business uses to do business.

The inside has to do with processes, manufacturing, the retail store stocking of shelves. The inside also has to do with administration, accounting, warehousing, inventory, and so on.

The front door is sales, marketing, advertising, delivery, accounts receivable, and so on.

Most businesses fit this model. If it's a manufacturing company they buy raw materials or semifinished goods, bring them in the back door, put them through a process in the inside, and sell them out the front door. If it's a retail store they buy goods, bring them in the back door, stock them on shelves on the inside, and advertise so that customers will come in the front door and buy. A consulting business brings knowledge in the back door, puts it into a usable format on the inside, and sells it to clients out the front door.

It is a division that helps me stay organized in the questioning process. The sales interview is a matter of give and take. The client hasn't read your script and so may take you off on many rabbit trails. The B.I.F model helps me be sure that I have covered every area.

I'll give you an example. A Georgia banker and I were making a joint call on a heating and air-conditioning construction contractor. Their specialty had been working with government buildings, such as hospitals, schools, jails, and courthouses, in a thirty or forty county area in central Georgia. The firm was over twenty-five years old and well established. They had a good reputation and a good working relationship with most of the general contractors who did this type of construction. In fact, they would often bid the same job through two or more general contractors and would therefore get the work no matter who got the bid.

We, of course, were looking for problems they might have that our bank could solve. We couldn't find any. They had been banking with the same bank, one of our competitors, for a number of years. We knew there had been some personnel changes at that bank, but it didn't seem to have affected our prospect's dealing with that bank.

The prospect was very open to telling us about his business. He showed us a courthouse plan he was bidding at the time. He even went on to tell us how overbuilt most government buildings are.

After an hour, we knew a lot about the business. We had asked all the questions I could think of and were about to wrap up. Then I pictured by B.I.F. model. My mind quickly reviewed my list of back door, inside, and front door questions. Suddenly one stood out that I did not have an answer for—discounts for quick pay to suppliers. I asked it.

"By the way, do your suppliers still offer a discount for quick pay on your accounts?"

"Yeah, they do. But you have to understand our business." I often have prospects explain their business to show its uniqueness. "Remember, our work is almost all government. We submit a bill to our general contractor on the first. He probably submits it by the tenth and the bureaucracy takes until at least the thirtieth before we get paid. If we paid our bills by the tenth we'd get a 2 percent discount, but that would tie up a lot of money so I guess I've always figured that 2 percent wasn't worth it."

I started to jot some notes on a blank sheet of my legal pad. "In other words," I said as I wrote, "you are paying your suppliers 2 percent to borrow money from them for twenty days." I showed him these notes.

30th − 10th = 20 days × 2%

"Is that right?" I asked.

"Yeah." He looked at the notes. "I never thought about it quite that way, but I guess that is what I'm doing."

"Have you ever figured the Annual Percentage Rate on that

borrowing?" I had gotten his attention. Then I wrote out these notes on the pad:

30th − 10th = 20 days × 2%

20 days into 360 = 18 × 2% = 36% APR

He looked at the notes. He said, "Wow! I'll have to think about that."

"We could charge you a pretty exorbitant rate on a revolving credit line at the bank and you would still come out ahead," I said laughing.

Later, as we were leaving, I reviewed our call with him verbally. I told him I really admired the way he was running his business and felt he had a good handle on his finances. "In fact," I said, "it seems the only financial problem you might not have addressed is the matter of not taking advantage of your discounts."

His agreement was a faint, "Hmmm."

A few months later I got a call from the banker with whom I had made the call. "Remember our contractor call, the guy who wasn't taking advantage of his 2 percent discounts?" I remembered. "Well, he is coming in this afternoon to open a revolving line of credit to take advantage of his discounts. I think we've got a good chance at getting the rest of his business." Eventually, they did.

Here are a few questions I have used in each of the three B.I.F categories. I'm sure you can think of more:

The Back Door:

Who are your suppliers?
Where are they located?
What does each provide you?
How do they ship?
Do they have backlogs?
What kinds of terms do they offer?
Do they offer discounts for prompt pay? Do you take advantage
   of these? If not, why?
How do they handle shipping?
Are there other possible providers? Why do you not use them?

Are there advantages to large lot shipping? Do you take advantage of these? Why or who not?

Can you save money by using your own trucks and picking up shipments? Do you? If not, why?

Inside:

What kind of facilities do you have? Could we take a tour? (if appropriate)

Are there any changes you would make if you could?

What equipment do you have?

What new equipment are you considering?

How many people do you have?

What are their functions?

Tell me about your organization.

Who handles your bookkeeping?

Do you use outside accounting?

Do you have computers? Should you?

What kind of inventory do you maintain?

Tell me about your benefits package? Is it adequate? What changes would you make if you could?

Front Door:

Who are your customers?

Where are they located?

How do you sell to them?

Do you have potential for growth?

Where is it?

What's preventing you from getting that business?

How do you sell your products (services)?

Tell me about your sales force.

What kind of training do you offer your sales force?

How are they compensated? Is that working?

Do you have trucks for delivery?

Do you furnish cars to your salespeople?

How about communications?

Do your salespeople have computers? Are they tied into the LAN?

Do they have car or portable phones? Beepers? How do you stay in touch?

If there were anything you could change about how your sales
  force operates, what would that be?
What advertising do you do? Where? How much?
Does your industry have trade shows and do you participate in
  them?

Many of these questions are geared toward people who sell such
services as banking and training. You may have to tailor your
questions to your product or services.

Also, these questions are for use when it is very necessary to
learn about the total business. Don't overlook the possibility that if
you broaden your questioning process you just might stumble onto
some problems you can solve that are outside of the ordinary scope.

Another trick I use to help organize my thinking is what I call
the "Road Map." I like to think of the sales interview as a journey. I
have a map with certain destinations in mind. These destinations
are my solutions (or products and services).

Just pretend for a moment that I have an airline that goes to
Dallas, Chicago, New York, Philadelphia, and Los Angeles. I begin
to sense that the prospect has a problem in Denver. I don't go there.
This is not a problem for which I have a solution, so I don't want to
follow that line of conversation too far. If I do I will get the prospect
motivated to go to Denver and I can't get him there. I have
frustrated the prospect and wasted time for both of us.

To put this in real terms, if I work for a bank and the prospect
begins to tell me about the problem of his roof leaking, I can't help
him, unless he needs financing for the repairs. I'm not in the
roofing business. I may be sympathetic to his problem but I don't
want to ask a lot of questions to get him motivated to solve the
leaking-roof problem. If I do, he may end up saying, "Excuse me. I'd
like to continue this conversation but I've got to get the roof
repaired."

I might steer the conversation away with a question like, "Let's
assume you get the roof problem solved and you still don't make
your deadlines for the Johnson contract. Is there any other problem
that might prevent your getting there?"

If the answer is no, then I either have to find a new direction or
say goodbye and let the prospect call the roofing company.

You can develop questions that will lead to the points on your Road Map with the following chart:

My product or service	Problems it solves	Questions that would flesh out one of these problems

Here are a few examples from my consulting business:

My Product or service	Problems it solves	Questions that would flesh out one of these problems
Sales training	Lack of sales per call	1. Tell me about your sales staff. 2. Are you satisfied with their performance? Why now? 3. What do you think might be the problem? 4. If they increased their performance by, say, 30 percent, what would that do for your bottom line?
Marketing planning	Not reaching a sufficient market	1. Tell me something about the sales history of the company. 2. What do you think you ought to be doing? 3. Tell me about your marketing approach, your advertising. 4. How do you feel about that? 5. If you could increase your market penetration by, say, 10 percent, what would that mean to your bottom line?

Management training	Problems in meeting deadlines	1. You mentioned problems in getting production out. Tell me about that. 2. Do you think you have good people who are capable of doing the work with proper management? 3. Is good management a problem for you? 4. Have you trained your managers and supervisors in how to manage?

Now if you do find the prospect heading toward a destination (problem) that is on your map, you want to continue to ask questions to flesh out the problem. Remember the process of behavior change. The prospect has to look closely at the problem, define it, feel its pain, and begin to want a solution. This takes time. You may be anxious to talk about a solution but the prospect probably needs to spend time looking at the problem. Your questions will help that process.

Obviously the questions we have talked about so far have applied to businesses that need to look at the total business in order to develop relationship and look for problems in the prospect's business. Your business may not be of that type. However, don't have too narrow a focus when asking questions.

No matter what your relationship might be with the customer on whom you are calling, a broad knowledge of his or her business may be helpful. Architects, CPAs, and engineers can all better fit their work into the background of a business as a whole.

Whenever I go to my doctor for some complaint she always asks me, "What's going on in your life, Dick?" This is a good question for a doctor. My body does not function in a vacuum. Probably the business problems you are trying to solve don't either. This certainly would be true if you are in a business such as security systems, air conditioners, office furniture, equipment, investments, and a lot more.

At any rate, remember that the motivation to buy your product or service will come from the prospect seeing that the product or service will help him reach his goals. You need to know at least a little about what those goals are. Your questions, at least early in the interview, should be structured to find out what some or all of those goals are. Besides, people like to talk about their businesses. And relationships are built on knowledge and understanding.

You often can find problems for which you have a solution by asking about the future. "Where do you expect to be this time next year? In two years? Five years?" When the prospect answers, ask, "Let's say it is next year and you haven't reached your goal. Do you anticipate any particular problems that might keep you from getting there?" If the prospect comes up with something you may be off and running with a problem that will lead to your solution.

Another time to bring goals back into the conversation is when you have found a problem and you are fleshing it out with questions. Ask the prospect how this problem is affecting his ability to reach his goals.

After you have thoroughly fleshed out a problem and you sense that the prospect is beginning to want a solution, ask a question such as, "If you solve that problem and reach the goal we have discussed, can you anticipate what that might mean in terms of dollars and cents added to your bottom line?" A firm answer here will be a big help in placing your product or service in terms of value for the cost. You might later find yourself saying, "Yes, our product is expensive but when you consider that its solving your problem could bring ten times its cost to your bottom line, the cost seems a lot more reasonable."

These principles work in almost any situation. Even if you are trying to sell your ideas to a boss or to a peer-level department head whose cooperation you need, he will be asking the question, "What's in it for me?" A thorough understanding of the goals and objectives of the person you're working with will go a long way toward making the sale.

Asking well-thought-out questions can do a lot for you in the sales interview. Not only will they impress the client with your interest and knowledge but they will also give you confidence in directing the conversation. Sometimes, particularly if you are beginning to use some new approaches in your selling, it helps to write out a list of good questions. You can put the list under the last page of your notepad. Then if you get to one of those embarassing pauses in your visit you can say, "I made a list of questions I wanted to be sure to get answers for. Would you mind if I went over my list to make sure I haven't left anything out?" Then look at your list and find a question you have forgotten. This shows planning and concern for the prospect.

Now, let's talk a little more about listening. Active listening is a skill. Not only do you have to focus your total thought process on listening to the prospect but you have to let him know that you are listening. A good listener has good eye contact. Of course, you must look away some to take notes, but this should be held to a minimum. A good listener will tilt his head to the side every so often as if to get a different slant on what is being said.

Feedback is a necessary indicator of listening. Repeating in your own words what has just been said is one way of giving feedback. Presenting the prospect's statement in the context of other businesses with which you have worked is also an excellent way of showing that you have heard what's just been said. It also give some indication of your experience with similar problems.

Verbal reinforcement is another good indicator of listening. An "I see" or just an "Uh-huh" shows the other person that you are receiving the information. It also tells the prospect that what he has just said my be important. Saying something like, "Really? Tell me about that" can get the prospect to expand on the subject. It may well help him uncover a problem that he had overlooked. With luck it will be a problem for which you have a solution.

Once, when I was calling on behalf of a bank, I had a prospect say, "Our business is seasonal. Consequently, in the summer, when we're really busy, our inventory is up, our accounts receivable is up, and we tend to have a pinch on our cash flow."

I countered with, "Really? Tell me about that."

He expanded. We got into a lot of the details. We soon were headed toward a line of credit, my solution to his problem. He had been living with the problem but had not focused on it enough to think in terms of a loan to get over the lean times. My questions and active listening got him to bring the problem into the forefront of his thinking, part of the process of behavior change.

At this point many people ask me, "Will they really tell you that much?" You may be wondering the same thing.

The answer is a resounding, "Yes." If your Call Purpose

Statement gives a good reason for your learning, if you ask good questions, if you listen and give feedback, your problem will be getting out of there on time for your next appointment. People love to talk about what they do. I always allow an hour and a half between appointments and I almost always use it up.

9

Please Understand Me

O.K. You've asked good questions. You've listened. You've nodded and ummed and hmmed in all the right places. And then, suddenly...Eureka! You've discovered a problem. It is the mother of all problems. And it is a problem for which you have the perfect solution.

"Let me tell you how we can solve that problem," you say.

Stop!

We're a long way from presenting the solution. Remember when the doctor was asking me questions about my back? He knew I had a problem with my back. Many doctors, and other salespeople, would have jumped right in to tell me their solution. Many doctors would have come into my room telling me about putting me in the hospital and what treatment they would prescribe, or at least what tests they would run.

But our good doctor Sadler did not do that. He started asking questions. As he asked those questions I began to understand my problem better and in the process became motivated to find a solution.

In my call with the banker in Georgia, I found a problem with the air-conditioning contractor not taking advantage of his 2 percent discounts. And you may have noticed in my call on the air-conditioning contractor that I did not immediately start pitching a revolving credit line to fix the problem. His answer would have been, "But you don't understand my business." Instead I asked more questions. I put the answers down on paper, redefined of course, to show the Annual Percentage Rate. He had to answer several of my questions before *he* began to understand that he had a problem. After I was sure that he understood in clear terms what his problem was, *then* and only then did I present a solution. And then I presented the solution in a rather casual manner. I knew he would have to think about it for a while. He was an analytical. They have to study a problem over time. Then, when it was his idea, he came to the bank to seek the solution that I had presented.

I had a banker tell me once that when bankers first learn to sell they work on the rapport-development step. He had been selling bank services successfully for a long time, but he had brought me into his bank to train the other bankers in selling skills. He told me, "These fellows are making a few calls. They've gotten the rapport-development step down pretty well. But they are so tickled to keep a conversation going that they spend thirty minutes developing rapport, then hand the prospect their card and say 'If I can ever help you let me know.' It's a waste of time."

After some training I finally got those bankers into a good Call Purpose Statement and they were amazed at how much they learned about the prospect's business. But my next problem was to keep them from jumping into a solution the minute they heard a problem. You see, the bankers were used to solving a problem when it was brought to them by a customer. They felt right at home presenting the solution. So when they spotted a problem in the conversation with the prospect, it was natural for them to start to solve it, even though the prospect had not had time to define and clearly understand his problem, and, more important, had not developed the motivation to seek a solution.

You may find that in your business. If you have been waiting for customers to come in with a problem that you know how to solve you probably jump right into your solution. That works fine inside your business because the customer has already been far enough through the problem/solution cycle to have felt the pain of his problem and is ready to hear a solution. That may not work when you are out making the call. This is true even if the customer has called and asked you to come to his place to discuss a problem. He still may not clearly understand his problem and may not yet be ready for a solution, particularly if it will cost more than he had considered.

In addition, the motivation from understanding his problem may not yet be in place. And, at any rate, the prospect has not had the experience of going through his problem with you so that he knows that *you* clearly understand his problem.

So, a good list of questions concerning the problems that you solve is a first priority. In the previous chapter I gave you a form for formulating questions about each of your solutions (products and/or services). Having this list of questions clearly thought out and ready is a primary skill in selling your solutions.

In the story about the doctor and my injured back, the doctor asked a lot of questions. Together we fleshed out my problem. In that process I came to understand my problem better. I also knew that the doctor now understood what was ailing me.

Now, you say, we're ready to tell the customer about our solution. Not so fast. There is one more critical step, the *Summary Feedback*. This the process of reviewing our understanding of the problem. The doctor did that in a few words, in which he fed back to me in his own words my answers to his questions. In other words, he reviewed with me my understanding of the problem.

Some magic happened. In the few seconds that it took to review the problem the doctor did several things. First, he checked out his understanding of the problem. He wanted to make sure that he had the problem down correctly, that he had listened well and had not made any mistakes or jumped to some conclusions that I had not followed. Second, he got me to review my problem. The process of going over my problem again further motivated me to seek a solution. He was also checking for indications that I was, indeed, ready to find a solution. Third, and probably the most important thing, he let me know that *he* understood and had listened. This last thing put him in the true role of a consultant. Together we had described and defined my problem. He was my partner, a partner in the discovery of the problem, and soon to be a partner in the seeking of a solution. We were a team.

Now I was ready for a solution and the doctor said, "Dick, I'm going to put you in the hospital and we'll run these tests and do some therapy and I think you'll be on your feet in a few days."

I said, "Let's go." I had forgotten about the seminar I was to give that week. Or at least its importance had dropped way down on my list of priorities. I was ready to take the next step in the cycle of behavior change and that was to make the changes necessary to find a solution to the back problem. It had become my first priority, and the price of the change, postponing my seminar in Odessa, seemed well worth the cost.

The Summary Feedback is so important in my walking through the cycle of behavior change with the prospect that I consider it a separate step. It is so important, in fact, that I often write it out and attach it to a written solution (proposal). I usually title it a "Summary of Understanding" or a "Background Summary."

In my written proposal I often ask the prospect to go over the "Summary" very carefully as the attached proposal is based on the accuracy of this understanding. I really do want the prospect to correct my mistakes, to point out any key factors that I might have omitted. If I have made mistakes I quickly correct them. People don't mind your making a mistake if they have a chance to correct it and see that you make the change. This process itself helps in building the problem-solving motivation.

Once a partner and I called on a major real estate developer that was a subsidiary of a Fortune 500 company. We had an interview with the vice president of marketing and his marketing manager. The interview lasted nearly two hours. My partner and I asked every question we could think of. We really got a handle on the situation and the problems. Following the lead of the *Fortune* 500 parent company, the development company moved its people around a lot, and this vice president had recently come into this job from another unrelated section of the business. He was new. He knew he had found a can of worms in this new job. He was looking for help.

As we were wrapping up our call we gave the vice president a shortened, verbal version of the Summary Feedback. He agreed that we seemed to have a good understanding of what he had found in this department. We then told him that we would come back in a few days with a written proposal.

When I called for an appointment to present our proposal the vice president suggested we meet over lunch. I don't like lunch calls for selling. The salad is always getting in the way of my taking notes or presenting written proposals. But I didn't feel like pressing the issue, so I agreed.

We had lunch at a fancy restaurant near the prospect's office. My partner and I had brought four copies of the "Background Sum-

mary and Proposal": one for the vice president, one for his
manager, and one for each of us. It was twelve pages long. Five of
those pages were taken up with the Background Summary.

After exchanging pleasantries we went over our process of
preparing the proposal, in which we explained the written Background Summary, how important it was to the correctness of the
proposal, and asked that they read it carefully. They did. The waiter
took our order. They read. The waiter brought our salads. They
read. They got a little ranch dressing on the proposal. My partner
and I turned a page whenever the vice president turned a page. We
were ready for questions or corrections.

The vice president punctuated his reading with "Uh-huh,"
"Yeah," "Boy, that's right," and "You really listened." Finally he
finished.

He looked me right in the eye and said, "This is the clearest
summary of the problems I have found here that I have seen. I wish
I had written it." Then he began to look at the proposal section.
"Now let's see how you've proposed to solve this mess." We, again,
followed him page by page through the proposal. We got the job.

But let's pause a minute and consider the position the prospect
was in as he considered our proposal. We had spent two hours with
him helping him define the problems he had found in his new
position. We not only had obviously understood these problems but
had documented our understanding in writing. In addition, we had
provided him with a working document to begin solving these
problems. Even if he had been considering some other consultants,
and he may have been, who do you think had the inside track? We
did, of course. We held his job in our hands. We had it in writing.
We had shown ourselves worthy of becoming partners with this
man in solving these problems. And, apparently, he thought so, too.

The written format of the Summary Feedback is time consum-
ing. Obviously, you would not take the time for a small job in which
the ratio of sales time to finished product is too high. But the power
of the document is immeasurable. It does many things. The first, of
course, is showing your understanding and concern for finding a
solution to your prospect's problem.

There are many other aspects to the written Summary Feedback.
It becomes a representative for you in the prospect's office. I once
left a written Summary Feedback and Proposal with a bank

marketing officer. I finally got the business but it was over a year later. I called the prospect a week after I had gone over the document with her. She had not been able to go over it with the president because he had left on vacation. I called back two weeks later as requested. The president had seen it but wanted the executive vice president for loans to review it. He was at a convention.

To make a long story a little shorter, that document went all over the bank. It was duplicated and shown to the board of directors. Whenever I called, the marketing officer always knew where the document was, whose desk it had migrated to at the time. Even though it took a year, my letterhead and proposal were there representing me in that bank. When I was finally hired and went in to do the work, one of the other officers said, "I'm glad I've finally met you. You were on my desk for six weeks."

And that brings up another point. Almost no one throws away a Summary Feedback report. They think they might need it sometime. Many times it is the only written history of the company and the situation. It has value to the organization.

As a consultant, of course, the Summary Feedback report shows my abilities at capturing and summarizing findings. That in itself is valuable. See if it might also apply to your work. But its main function is to show your understanding of the problem and that you care. It obviously takes time and effort, and that shows the prospect that you take his problems seriously.

It does take time. However, it may surprise you to learn how little time it really does take, particularly after you've written a few. For the most part it is merely organizing and writing out your notes. If you've taken careful notes it is almost written for you.

Here is an example of a Summary Feedback I actually used. I have changed the company name to Generic and changed some of the details to protect the confidentiality of my client:

Background Summary

Founded in 1978 and specializing in outpatient health-care services, Generic, Inc., is a multiregional provider of intravenous therapy and nursing care for patients at home. The Company's ultimate goal is to become a large, profitable national player in the home-health-care arena, a field which promises to become a $45 billion market by the year 2000. The following additional information seems pertinent to our study:

- A quote from an industry magazine states that: "Volume gains will be dramatic, fed by new applications of existing therapies, advances in infusion pump technology, and patients in a broadening number of diagnostic groups now viewed as suitable candidates for alternate-site care."

- The Company has its headquarters in Atlanta. The Company's marketing focus has centered in the major communities with offices concentrated in Atlanta, Macon, Savannah, Columbus, Mobile, Jackson, and the Mississippi Gulf Coast.

- New capital was infused into the Company in 1987 and the aggressive program of acquisition was stepped up. On October 1, 1990, the Company acquired First Home Care, Inc. The pro forma revenue for the combined companies of 1989 was about $22.5 million with a net loss of some $100 thousand. However, Generic itself showed a net profit in excess of $900,000 for the fourth quarter of 1989, reversing a year-long loss trend. Several cost saving steps initiated in 1989, including the closing of four offices in Colorado, helped in this turnaround.

- In June of 1991 the Company acquired Second Care, Inc., with headquarters in Orlando. This gave the company a total of 36 offices in Georgia, Alabama, and Mississippi.

- An outstanding mission statement was developed this year. It has been featured in the Company's annual report for 1990 and has been widely disseminated to all company personnel.

- The Company has a staff of sales personnel who talk to doctors and other referral sources, such as insurance companies, about the services offered. However, once a patient is referred the staff nurses and pharmacists continue the interface with the referral.

- Tom Jones, Vice President for Operations, feels that most of the staff are good technically and meet the needs of both the patients and the referrers from a technical standpoint.

However, each contact is an opportunity to cross-sell additional services for the Company and Jones feels that the staff professionals may be missing these opportunities.

- The Company has a total of some 2,400 employees. Of these, perhaps three to four hundred would fall into the category of interfacing with the referrals. The collections staff has to interface with the clients but their focus is collection, therefore cross-selling opportunities are different.

- The Company has an internal education department but their primary focus in the past has been technical. Donna Kincaid, Director of Professional Services, has excellent background in sales for the Company and could probably work with the implementation of any new training program.

- Of all of the Company personnel, Jones feels that one operations manager in one of the Mississippi offices is the most customer-oriented. Perhaps she could be used as a role model for any training.

- Jones wants a training program to focus on the sales and customer relations aspects of the business for those professionals who have referral interface. He also wants a general training program to teach customer relations standards to the entire staff. His current goal is to have a companywide program in place by year-end 1991.

Objectives

Based on our conversations it seems safe to assume the following objectives for the training program:

1. To develop a companywide "response style" for all customer contacts.

2. To develop a training program that instills this response style in *all* personnel, including new hires.

3. To develop a business extension attitude on the part of *all* customer contact personnel, including new hires.

4. To develop a training program that instills this attitude.

5. To institute an initial training program that accomplishes these objectives within a budget appropriate to the current profit level of the Company.

6. To develop a training program that will lend itself to expansion into video support at a later date as the training budget expands.

This one is fairly short but it covers the pertinent information that sets up the problem. In this case I did get a copy of the most recent annual report and some of the information came from that source. Learning to read an annual report or other financial data is important in the banking and consultant businesses. It may be in yours. At any rate it never hurts to ask for such reports as well as product and service literature.

This particular company had a problem when they called me. They were referred to me by a mutual friend. The friend had been consulting with them in the area of recruiting and hiring new employees. Tom Jones thought he had a good handle on the problem when he called. He knew I was in the training/consulting business and knew a little about my background. Still, I used a Call Purpose Statement that gave me a reason to take a broad look at the company.

I have used one format in this Summary Feedback to the health-care company. There are many different ways of organizing the material. I have some clients that put the information in a letter format.

One banker who went through my seminar told me that he would lay his notes out on the car seat after leaving a call and dictate a Summary Feedback into his portable dictating machine while negotiating big-city traffic. He showed me some examples. They were a mess, mostly one long jumbled paragraph. However, he reported fantastic results and comments from his prospects. The prospects were so impressed to have a banker record their business that the format was unimportant. (I wonder about the banker's driving record, too.)

In the objectives section in the example above, notice that I preface it with "Based on our conversations it seems safe to assume the following objectives." In this case the prospect and I had not clearly defined the objectives: at least we did not call them that. However, we obviously talked about what he wanted to accomplish. I had notes to back up my assumptions. Since we did not clearly state that these were objectives, I used the "assumption" sentence so as not to presume too much. At any rate there will be plenty of time to check out the accuracy of my assumptions later. Most prospects appreciate having their objectives stated in writing.

Also, in this example I have left out a special section on problems. The word *problem* has a harsh tone in print and, unless the prospect has used that word rather emphatically, I hesitate to write it down. I will, sometimes, use the term *areas of concern*. This has a softer ring and is a little more palatable.

There are times when there are additional divisions that need to be addressed. For instance, you might entitle the whole document "Summary of Understanding." Then you can subtitle the first section "Background Summary," another section "Competition," and still a third section "Marketing." The section titles can be changed to fit your particular business and information.

In writing the Summary Feedback I usually lay out my legal-pad notes and mark them according to my sections. For instance, I might mark them "B" for background, "C" for competition, "M" for marketing, and "O" for objectives. At that point my organization is half done. Then I write them out in narrative form one section at a time, marking through the notes as I use them. This way I don't leave anything out. With the magic of a word processor the notes can then be reorganized within each section so that the most important items are first and there is a logical sequence. With a little practice the whole process can be complete in less than thirty minutes.

Here is another example of a Summary Feedback. I borrowed this from a client of mine who has found the written feedback to be invaluable. My client is in the business of managing oil-field holdings for third parties. Here he believes that his firm can operate certain wells for another company more productively than the prospect. I have, of course, disguised the names and some of the details to protect anonymity.

The proposal followed in the same letter. The Summary Feedback is an absolutely necessary part of the sales interview. It can be a few seconds of verbal reciting of the prospect's situation at the

PERSONAL AND CONFIDENTIAL

Mr. John Doe
Doe Exploration Company
1234 Any Street
Anytown, Texas

Re: Background Summary and Proposal to Provide Services

Dear John:

It was a pleasure meeting with you last week to learn more about what Doe Exploration is doing. It's good to see you so relaxed. The vacation must have been good for you.

The following represents our understanding of Doe's present situation:

1. You have sold substantially all of your operated properties to other energy companies, primarily XYZ Corporation. You still operate eight wells, of which four are currently active. Two of the inactive wells have work planned, including the Johnson and Williams #8.

2. Doe still owns substantial other nonoperated oil and gas assets through Jesse Oil and Gas Co., and has interest in an Illinois gas field and gathering system. Doe also has an interest in a production barge rented to Jackson Oil & Gas Co., Inc.

3. You are planning to dispose of your current hardware package and invest in a personal-computer–based networked system. You are evaluating current staffing levels based on expected activity levels. You would like to minimize overhead.

4. Doe is evaluating a reentry into oil and gas exploration and has a prospect in North Alabama waiting on a farm out from a Major. You are actively consulting other exploration prospect generators to find out what they are doing to refine your approach.

5. You are also looking for good investments while reformulating your plans.

6. You would like to consider turning operation of the remaining wells over to a firm like Generic Services, Inc.

Based upon our discussion, we assume that Doe's corporate objectives are:

1. Evaluate the opportunities available to raise money for oil and gas exploration and once a niche is determined, reenter the market.

2. Minimize overhead associated with operations.

3. Monitor and administer current investments with a lean staff.

close of the call or it can be written, or both. In fact, there should be some verbal expression of summary at the end of each call. It ties up the loose ends and shows the prospect or client that you have heard and understood. It definitely should precede any presentation of a solution.

Thus, assuming that you make a sale in one call, you would present the Summary Feedback verbally before presenting the solution.

In a brief sales call in which the sale is consummated all in one visit, your Summary Feedback might sound like this if you are selling a plant and flower rental service:

"Mr. Prospect, let me make sure I've understood what you've said. Your company has been in business over twenty-seven years.

You've been in this new building now for nearly eighteen months. In the old building you had atriums and most of your plants were actually in the ground in the atrium. You had a vice president who was partially retired who loved to care for the plants.

"In the new building you have no atrium, the vice president has fully retired and moved away, and you've tried caring for plants in pots but they have all died. All you your employees miss the plants from the old building and you feel that plants add a lot not only to the morale of your employees but that good plantings in the reception and office area is an added benefit to your customers. Is that a pretty good summary of where I've found you?"

The prospect might say something like, "Yes. And don't forget that *I* just like having plants around and I'm really frustrated that they have all died." He's working with you to establish the proper background for your proposal.

Now let's look at some additional benefits to a written Summary Feedback. There are many.

For one thing, a written Summary Feedback gives you a document describing your prospect and, later, customer. It can stay in their permanent file. It can be updated as the relationship grows.

It is an excellent document to use for informing others in your organization about the prospect or customer. I have referred back to a client Summary Feedback several years after I have worked with him. It brings my memory of the client to the front of my mind. Often the client enjoys going over bits of his history that he has long since forgotten.

Information in the Summary Feedback is good for the credit department. It serves as a good background document for the credit file. It can even give good research information should there be a credit problem. Credit people love it.

After the sale is made and the relationship established, the Summary Feedback can be distributed to any and all personnel who will be working with the new client. In a few short minutes they can share in the initial interview and by giving feedback to the client can piggyback on that relationship.

A technician who is assigned to the new client may well start his introductory visit to the client's office with, "I've gone over our Summary of Understanding, which was attached to the original proposal. I'd like to go over a few of the items to make sure I have a clear understanding." It's a great shortcut to relationship building for all who follow.

Sales based on relationships are seldom made on the first call. In fact, one study reported that the average number of calls to make a sale of this type is five. Many of these second, third, or more calls involve a second or even a third person. The Summary Feedback instrument is a great tool for involving the new person.

"Hi, Joe. I'd like you to meet Bob Lewis. You remember I told you on our last call that your particular problem required some special expertise. Well, Bob here is the expert I was telling you about that knows everything about that application. I was sharing some ideas from my last call and he had a lot of questions that I couldn't answer. I hope you don't mind my bringing him along."

"No that's fine. The more the merrier. If we can get the problem solved I'm all for the help."

"Well, Joe, I wrote out a summary of your situation as I understand it from my last call. I have shared that with Bob. As I said, he had some questions I couldn't answer. But just to make sure I've given him a clear picture, why don't you go over this summary and check for mistakes or anything I might have left out. I brought a copy for each of us. We'll just follow along and if we need to add something just say so."

All three of us sit and read to ourselves. There may or may not be any corrections or additions. If there are Bob and I quickly correct ours and we continue.

At the end of the reading it becomes very obvious that Bob is now included in the group. I have brought him into the relationship almost as if he had been in on the initial interview.

The Summary Feedback, be it short and verbal or long and written or both, is a critical step in the sales process. And there is one more secret to it—your competition isn't using it. I've been preaching this process for almost twenty years. Very few have heard the call.

There are a number of professions that use a similar document: a banker's loan agreement, a lawyer's brief, a letter of intent, even a letter of agreement. But it is usually to clarify an already concluded relationship. I know very few people who make use of it in a selling situation.

Try it. You'll like it. It's extremely ethical, nonmanipulative, and only takes a little time.

10

We've Solved This Problem Before

YOU are finally ready to make your presentation. This time may have come during your first call or may well be two, three, or even six calls later. We are building a relationship and that takes time.

Let's assume for the moment that your first call has gone well. You have learned about your prospect's business. You have developed a good relationship. You have discovered one or more problems that you think you can solve. You have given a good verbal Summary Feedback. You are now ready to present your solution.

You might close your Summary Feedback with a question, "Do you feel I have a pretty good understanding of your situation?" If the answer is, "Yes. You've really helped me get a handle on the problem. I think you've got as good an understanding as I could possibly expect."

You answer, "Good. Would you be interested in how we have solved similar problems for many hundreds of our other clients?" At this point your prospect will undoubtedly want to hear more.

On the other hand, one of our good analytical friends might still be hesitant. He or she might say, "Well, you've given me a lot to think about. I didn't really realize the magnitude of my problem. Let me think about it for a while and then let's talk some more." This is your exit cue. Take it. Our analytical really needs time to think. You might set a time to call back. But leave. That will gain the analytical's respect. Then call back on the exact date you said you would.

The other three styles (driving, amiable and expressive) are probably going to want to hear your solution. Even the analytical might want to hear the solution to add to his pool of thought. So at any rate, you have a willing audience for your solution presentation.

Here are a few basic rules to remember in presenting the solution:

1. It is a solution. Think of it not as your service or product but as the solution to the problem you have just defined.
2. Put yourself in the prospect's shoes. If you were hearing this for the first time what would you want to hear?
3. Talk about benefits before features. Benefits are the ways in which your product or service solves the customer's problem. Features are how it works or what it does. The customer may want to know about the features eventually, especially the analytical customer. But he first wants to know how it will solve his problem.
4. Don't abandon the skills you have developed in helping clients at your place of business. Essentially the prospect is now almost at the same point as the client who walks in your door, problem in hand. Trust yourself.

A thought to keep in mind when making your presentation comes from B. C. Forbes, editor-in-chief of *Forbes* magazine from 1917 to 1954. This quote appeared in that magazine's December 5, 1994, edition, on page 314, in an article entitled "Thoughts on the Business of Life." He said, " 'D' ye think I'm in business for my health?' How often have you heard that? Every time I hear it I conclude that the man doesn't know what he is in business for. What are we in business for? We are in business to benefit others. If we are not, then our business won't prosper permanently. All business is a matter of reciprocity, of giving something in exchange for something else. Unless we give, we cannot receive. And the man or concern that gives us most naturally gets most in return. He reaps most who serves most. The most notably successful businesses are those that have rendered signally valuable services to the people."

Before we move on to getting the business, let's look at presentations that we make on the second, third, or later calls. We have time to prepare. Maybe we have the proposal in writing. If it's a big sale and a long-term relationship, we may well have the Summary

Feedback attached to a long and detailed proposal. My proposals for training programs to my client fit this criteria, so I'll use this as an example. The approach fits a lot of product and service solutions. If it fits yours, fine. If not I will try to show ways in which the concepts can apply to a broader range of products and services.

Presenting your solution to a client's problem is much like any other presentation you might make. The principles apply to a presentation of services, a speech to the PTA, an update meeting of your staff, or any other situation in which you are attempting to convey information or illicit a response. In teaching clients to make better presentations I find that most presenters focus on the presenting rather than the planning, whereas if the planning process is done correctly the presentation itself usually falls into place. So here I will give you some guidelines for planning a presentation:

1. Set a goal.
2. Analyze the audience.
3. Plan the opening and closing.
4. Plan the content.
5. Plan the audience participation.
6. Plan the environment.
7. Plan the audiovisuals.
8. Plan the request for action.

This sounds complicated, doesn't it? It really isn't. Some at this point may think it is too involved, too hard. Others, though, may think that they do this naturally. If you are in this latter group you may want to skip this next part. But perhaps even for you this might be a good review.

If you are trying this for the first time, a concerted and lengthy effort may be necessary. However, with time the process becomes almost automatic. Whether you are planning your presentation back at the office or just stepping into a presentation during the call, these steps will go through your mind and the end result will be far more effective. Making this eight-step plan part of your thought process takes time. I suggest you make the concerted effort a few times in order to make the process a habit.

Let's take the steps one at a time. The first is probably the most important. What is my goal? What do I want to happen because I made this presentation? Goal setting works. In at least a few of my eighteen years in business I have taken my own advice and written out goals for the year in December or January. Invariably, as I review my goals at the end of the next year I find that I have reached almost all of them. I have exceeded some. The details may be different but the end results are about as planned. The same is true for short-term goals set for a presentation. Goals work.

In his classic work *Psycho-cybernetics*, Maxwell Maltz, M.D., tells us that our subconscious mind is really a servo-mechanism much like a heat-seeking missile. We set the target and our subconscious goes to work helping us reach it. It will constantly make little adjustments as it sees us veering off-target.

Some sales trainers suggest the setting of a goal for a first sales call. While I agree this can be helpful in focusing our mind on a specific outcome, I am careful not to make my initial goal too specific as this might keep me from hearing the prospect's real problem. For instance, if a banker sets a goal of selling a particular type of loan to a client he might miss hearing that the client's real problem is money management and not a need for a loan at all. If I set a goal for a first call it tends to be rather broad, such as finding a problem for which I have a solution.

I had a banker friend who used to call this "something to hang my hat on." That banker would make a note of this problem beside the name of his prospect. Then, every quarter when our bank put out its quarterly report, he would send a copy to the prospect with some comment about the prospect's problem, perhaps an article the banker had read that gave a solution or showed how others had solved it. These little notes kept our banker uppermost in the mind of the prospect as a good source for solutions. It also showed an ongoing concern for the prospect.

But back to our presentation. How do we develop a goal? First let's review some basic rules for goal setting. To be effective, a goal must meet the following criteria:

> *It must be specific:* To say my goal is to make a customer out of the prospect is not specific enough. It must state an exact action, such as his buying a fifteen month training program to bring his sales staff up to top proficiency.
>
> *It must be measurable.* The goal above meets that criterion.

When I get to the end of the time period, can I measure the result? Count it in dollars? Measure the activity? Hold the signed contract in my hand?

It must be met within a specific period of time: I must set a date for the accomplishment of the goal. I want the prospect to buy the program for implementation during the next eighteen calendar months. Then at the end of the time period I can look at my calendar and look at the goal and see whether or not I have reached it. A goal without a time period is ongoing and I might always consider that I can reach it sometime in the future. It is not really a goal.

It must be challenging: If the goal is too easy, then there is no magic to inspire me to achieve it. Human beings need to stretch. I must see the goal as taking that extra effort, pushing me, stretching me.

It must be realistic: If a goal is too hard or unrealistic, then I may give up before I try. I have to believe the goal is achievable or I won't try. I may think I'm trying but my subconscious won't lock onto the target.

The art of goal setting lies between these last two criteria: setting a goal that will challenge one and thus provide adequate motivation but that is believably within reach.

Now that we know the rules, where does the goal come from? The answer is, in the future. What will the future look like if you reach the goal? What will the client relationship be if you make the sale? If you can state that clearly, even write it down, then you know what you want the prospect to do in order to fulfill that vision of the future.

So setting a goal is really asking the question, "What do I want to happen because I made this presentation? How will things be different? What will the client do that he would not otherwise do?"

You might say that it is obvious that you want to make a sale. But what does that mean? What is a "sale" for your business? I can't answer that, but you can. Is there the beginning of a relationship? If so, describe it. Is there just an exchange of money for a product? Then describe that. Your goal might be as simple as delivering and installing a new chlorinating system or as complicated as becoming the client's sole provider of architectural services for the twenty new projects the client has in mind over the next ten years. But whatever it is, write it down. A written goal has power. Your subconscious mind gets involved when you write.

Take time to write out your goal for the first few presentations you make and the goal-setting process will become a part of you. Then when it is time to present, even on the first call, your mind will work through the goal-setting process almost automatically.

The second step in preparing for the presentation is to analyze the audience. Some might say that this should come first, but I feel they have to come almost at the same time. Differences in your audience may well affect the goal you set. Yet knowing the goal may affect what aspects of the audience you analyze. Suffice it to say that they are both important and should be done simultaneously.

A written analysis of the audience can really be helpful. Granted, you may not have time to do this if the sale is about to take place on the first call. But if you take the time to write out the analysis a few times, again, the subconscious will take over in the short-term situations.

If you are making the presentation with others in your company or if others are involved, use them to help you with the analysis. This is especially true for those prospects where more than one of you has made one or more calls. Working together can develop a synergy. One of you may have noticed something that the other missed. At any rate, if you have to make the presentation together, analyzing the audience together will help you get the game plan developed so that you are on the same page during the presentation.

So what do you analyze? First, who will be there? Don't assume that just because nothing has been said there won't be new faces at the presentation. I made a call the other day to review my proposal and when I got to the company there were five people in the room. I knew only one. The proposal was for one branch of the company, but that branch manager had invited the other branch managers since he thought they, too, might want to use my services. The analysis of the audience must take into consideration the appearance of others that you don't know. At least ask yourself the question, "Who else is apt to be there and what can I assume about them?"

On page 121 is a form that will be helpful in the audience

Audience Analysis Worksheet

Name _____   **NOTES**

1. Background: Age _____ Sex _____

   Education _____

   Work Experience _____

2. Job in the company:

3. Individual objectives:

   _____

4. Knowledge level:

   _____

5. Income level:

6. Potential problem: Stumbling block:

   _____

   Question they might ask: _____

   _____

   What they might say: _____

7. Style: _____

8. Other comments: _____

   _____

   _____

   _____

analysis. Fill out one for each of the audience members. There may be other facts that you know about your audience or facts you would like to know. Add these to the form.

You may not have all of the information, but a good guess is better than nothing. You might mark the guesses so that you don't take them for facts. Guessing can be amazingly accurate and can tell you things you need to know. This is particularly true if several in your company who know the prospects discuss it.

You will notice in the form above that there is a place to put in style. Knowing the individual style of the audience members can be of great value when planning the content of your presentation, even the format and audiovisuals. When analyzing style, it really helps to discuss your thoughts with others even if they do not know the prospect. A second or third party can add objectivity and help you come up with a response that is less influenced by emotion.

The best way to analyze style is by taking one element at a time. In other words, look at the assertiveness axis (see chapter 6) first. Where does our prospect fall on the continuum? At this point pay attention to body language, movement, speed, eye contact, volume and tone of voice, and directness. Once you have your prospect placed on the assertiveness scale look at the responsiveness (the emotional openness) scale. Is he a cool, aloof, formal, expressionless person or a warm, friendly, open, people-type person who smiles and laughs easily. If you are still unsure then ask yourself about conversational elements. Does he talk about facts, tasks, and numbers, or does he talk about people and feelings.

Personal style will tell you a lot about buying style. Remember, analyticals and amiables are slow to decide and drivers and expressives make faster decisions. There are other factors that affect buying style that we will discuss later, but these are some guidelines.

Age, education, and income level are all factors in how people hear and receive a sales presentation.

Let's take the example of the architectural firm that has been asked to bid on the design of an adult retreat center at a summer camp owned by a presbytery. The presbytery is a political body made up of some 118 Presbyterian churches in a multicounty area. The project of building the retreat center has been assigned to a five-person committee made up of one minister and four laymen from churches throughout the presbytery.

One of the principals from the architectural firm and a staff member have met with the committee. They asked lots of questions about the new center—how it will be used, who will use it, how many people it should accommodate, the number of motel-type bedrooms, the level of the accommodations, etc. They have made a trip to the location, which is a hilly and heavily wooded site some seventy miles north of the presbytery's only major metropolitan area. They took enough measurements to make a reasonable layout back at the office.

The committee has asked that they bring a rough layout and ideas based on the current knowledge along with their own estimate of the cost of the project. The committee has told them that the presbytery has just under $1.5 million set aside for the project and will have to raise or borrow any additional money. No limits were set on the cost of the project but the architects were told that the presbytery is reluctant to make long-range commitments on borrowed funds and that the committee's fund-raising abilities will be limited.

The principal in the firm has assigned two of his best young architects to the project, and they have developed a plan to take advantage of the rather steep hills and beautiful woods. The committee suggested an auditorium capacity of 250 with sleeping accommodations for sixty in the beginning, as some of the dormitories from other parts of the camp could be used short-term. The architects designed a meeting room to accommodate 400 with breakout rooms for smaller groups.

The young architects proposed thirty sleeping rooms that would be about the level of a good motel. They laid out plans for additional sleeping rooms on the site that would eventually accommodate 400, with thirty to sixty room units being added in stages.

They met with the principal to plan the presentation. Their goal was to sell the idea of their approach even though their estimate of the cost was in excess of $2.5 million. Here was the goal they set and the way they analyzed the audience.

Their primary goal, of course, was to get the contract for the design and construction phases of the project. However, they felt that if they could get the committee to accept their more elaborate plans then getting the contract would be easy. So they set as their primary goal for the next presentation the acceptance of their proposed plan.

They then began the analysis of the audience. The principal and his staff associate who were at the first meeting met with the two young architects who had been assigned to the project. They discussed each member of the committee. The project architects asked some questions of those who had met the client.

There was the chairwoman, Helen, a housewife, whose husband had taught architecture at the local university and was now retired. The husband was not a member of the official committee but came to the meetings whenever his wife requested. He had not been at the meeting with the principal of the architectural firm.

After some discussion the group decided that the client chairwoman was analytical in style. She smiled rather easily when greeting people but when talking business she seemed very serious and thoughtful. She talked about facts, money, and numbers rather than people or feelings. She was dressed very conservatively.

The most outspoken member of the client committee was a Presbyterian minister named Bob. Bob was the one to greet the principal and associate when they came into the meeting. He had a firm handshake and a ready smile. He talked loudly and was very animated. His talk was of people, feelings, gaining consensus, and so on. Even though he was not the chairperson, he introduced the architects to each of the committee members, offered them coffee, and made them feel at home. Within the first few moments they knew all about Bob's church, the fact that he had been a minister for thirty-three years, and that he had three daughters and five grandchildren. Bob was clearly an expressive.

A third member, Jim, was a chemical engineer. He had worked for a large company for many years but took an early retirement and now had a very successful private consulting practice. In response to questions, Jim would pause for a long time, look at the floor with his hand to his chin, and think. Then he would carefully phrase his answer. The answers were clear and direct but diplomatic. The group decided Jim was an analytical with some driver tendencies.

The group went on with the analysis. They filled out the forms on each one. At the end of the planning session they had a clear feeling for the type of audience with which they were dealing. Basically, with the exception of Bob, the minister, the group tended to be conservative and analytical for the most part. The group of architects discussed the fact that the Presbyterian church as a whole tends to be analytical, even though some of its members, like Bob, may represent one of the other styles. Most organizations and businesses tend to have one of the four basic styles as a characteristic. Knowing the style of the organization or, in this case, the organization and the buying committee, will go a long way in helping to plan the presentation.

Feeling relatively comfortable with the analysis of the audience, the group of architects then went on to the next step in the planning process—planning the opening.

The opening of any presentation is the "grabber." It gets the audience's attention. It sets the mood and the pace for the presentation. Many sales are made or broken based on the opening of the presentation.

There are a number of good openers for presenting your solution. One of my favorites is a story. Everyone loves a story. This is particularly true if it is a story that they can relate to, one about someone in their situation. So a good way to open your presentation is by telling a story of someone else who had a similar problem to your prospect. The story, of course, has to have a happy ending, the solving of their problem made with your product or service. The story should be quick and to the point. And it should be true.

Another way to open a presentation is with a joke. Only tell a joke if it is relevant, can be tied to the problem/solution situation, and if you can tell a good one. There is nothing worse than a joke told by someone who can't tell one. This is especially true if the joke is not funny or doesn't fit the situation.

There is the historical approach, how we got in the business, if it applies to our problem/solution situation at hand. Perhaps you got into your business because you recognized that businesses had the kinds of problems for which you are currently proposing a solution. Telling a little about your background in founding your business, getting your education, or in some way preparing for this work might be appropriate.

The historical approach might also include an update since your last meeting. Or it might even cover the way in which your company or group went about proposing the solution—the research you did or the brainstorming.

And, of course, reviewing the Summary Feedback can also be used as the opening. You might begin by saying, "Since we understand that your problem was _____ we put our best heads to work on finding a solution. This one was unique. We wanted to make sure we had the very best solution. These are the people we had working on it and here is a little about their background and expertise."

In general, an opening should prepare your prospect for the solution to follow. It should summarize what you are going to tell him and might even hint at what is going to be requested. If appropriate, let him know what he has to gain from the presentation.

As with the entire presentation, the opening should take into account the style of the prospect. If you choose to tell a joke to an analytical you might get a polite smile. If it is really funny you might get a chuckle. If it is inappropriate, the drivers and analyticals might see it as being frivolous and unprofessional.

Analyticals might well be interested in how you arrived at the recommended solution. Drivers will want to get to the point, perhaps even the cost. They will interrupt and help move the presentation along. You need to plan for that.

Amiables are interested in the problem/solution story, particularly if they know the third party or can easily relate the third party to someone they know.

The expressive might like the joke. A few well-aimed remarks about the expressive's work and accomplishments will usually go over well.

The next step is planning the closing. You might ask why this would come next. The answer is that if we know what our close will be we know a good bit about what we will have to put in the body of the presentation in order to reach that ending.

The close should do three things: summarize the presentation, show the relevance to the situation, and ask for action. A story here is sometimes appropriate if it fits, if it is true, and if it is short and to the point. We will delve into this aspect of the presentation as we talk about asking for the business in a later chapter.

The body of the presentation is much more geared to your

particular business and your product or service. However, there are some general guidelines for planning it. First, be sure that it is presented in a way that shows clearly how it will solve the problem of the prospect. Often we can get so wrapped up in what we do for a living that we think everyone wants to know about it. They don't. They want their problem solved. So it helps to put yourself in the shoes of the prospect as you plan the presentation. What does he want to know? Can he easily see that the solution presented will really solve *his* problem and help *him* reach *his* goals?

Two other approaches for planning the presentation are the historical approach and the problem/solution approach. These two often overlap. The historical approach might include how you got into the business, why you do what you do, and how your business has evolved as you have worked with other clients. It is difficult to take this approach without getting into the problem/solution approach, how we have solved other similar problems for other clients. At any rate the third-party story of how this solution has worked for other clients is a must.

Once you have organized the content, know what you are going to say and how you are going to present it, you should then plan the amount of time the presentation will take. There are several factors that affect this aspect of the planning.

The amount of planning: In general the more carefully you have planned and rehearsed the presentation the more accurate your time estimate will be.

Your familiarity with the subject: The more familiar you are with the subject the more apt you are to add to the presentation as you go along. Therefore, time estimates tend to be short. Allow for this in your planning. I have had many partners and clients who think they can wing this part of the presentation simply because they know it so well. What often happens then is that the presentation gets too involved, takes too much time, and the client has to get on with other work and loses interest in the information you are giving. Planning is critical.

Use of written outlines or following a written proposal, handout materials, and the use of audiovisuals: All help to give more accuracy to time estimates.

A major factor in timing, of course, is the amount of time you think the prospect will give you for the meeting. If you have a good time estimate, ask for that amount of time when you set up the meeting. Plan your presentation for shorter than the time allowed. Then there will be time for questions and discussion. You want the prospect involved in the presentation. Besides, it never hurts to finish early.

A few words about audiovisuals: some people use them, some people don't. I don't much but probably should. It has been said that people remember 8 percent of what they hear and 20 percent of what they hear *and* see. So why do we not take advantage of that extra 12 percent? By the way, I am convinced that people remember over 80 percent of what they hear, see, and say. That's why the part after this section deals with audience participation.

Computers are becoming a really fine tool for making presentations. There are, first of all, many good, rather inexpensive laptops on the market. Many of these use color. For presentations these can usually be hooked up to a color monitor or there are devices you can buy to hook them directly to a color TV.

In lieu of this, screens can be printed out for overhead transparencies and used in this manner.

I'm not much of a computer expert but I have had years of experience with other media, so I'll give you some quick guidelines about flip charts, overheads, and slides.

Flip charts:

1. Advantages:
   a. They are usually readily available in most companies. If not, they are inexpensive and portable.
   b. They are versatile. They can be preprinted, even professionally, or written on as the presenter talks.
   c. They save the material covered.
   d. They provide a good focus for groups of up to thirty.
   e. Pages can be removed and saved or taped to the wall for future reference.
2. Guidelines:
   a. If material is preprinted, cover each page with two blank pages for opacity; on each page cover those items not yet discussed and uncover them as you go.
   b. Use watercolor markers. Permanent markers bleed through and make the following page look dirty.

c. Use several colors. They add interest and emphasis. Orange, yellow, and some reds and blues don't show up well.

d. Plan ahead if you wish to write items on the board as you talk. If you plan to put diagrams on the board, pencil them in lightly ahead of time to make sure you have enough room on the sheet.

e. If you have questions or discussion from group members, writing their comments on the flip chart reinforces their participation and gives clarity to the discussion.

f. If you have a lot of material to present, tear off each page as you go and have someone put it on the wall with masking tape.

3. Disadvantages:

a. The flip chart can have a homemade look to it. Having someone who can print well fill in the pages ahead of time can overcome this.

b. The flip chart is not good for groups of more than thirty. It is hard for those in the back to see. An overhead projector will do better for larger groups.

Overhead projector

1. Advantages:

a. The overhead projector has been called the electric flip chart. It can be used in much the same way. I've already mentioned that printouts from a computer can be put on acetate sheets for use with the overhead.

b. As mentioned above, it is much better for groups of more than thirty.

c. As opposed to slides, etc., it can be used in a fully lighted room.

d. Because you can turn it off and on, you can control the focus of the participants.

2. Guidelines:

a. Have plenty of blank acetate sheets on hand.

b. Use colored markers for emphasis. Again, the lighter markers don't show up well, so use them for highlighting only.

c. Have an extra bulb handy. They burn out at the darndest times.

   d. Preprinting can improve the professionalism of your
      presentation.
3. Disadvantages:
   a. The overhead projector images can also look homemade.
      Having preprinted sheets will help.
   b. Unlike the flip chart, you can display only one page at a
      time. You can bring a page back to look at it again, but the
      pages cannot be displayed around the room like flip chart
      pages.
   c. Some presenters have a problem looking at the bright light
      while they write. It takes some practice to write on the
      acetate sheets without looking directly at them.

Slides

1. Advantages:
   a. Slides can be very colorful and appealing. Good cameras
      are available now so that even amateurs can take excellent
      pictures to illustrate points.
   b. There are services available that will make all kinds of
      printed slides with charts and illustrations relatively inex-
      pensively. Computer programs are available for this, also.
   c. Preprepared slides give a presentation an air of profession-
      alism and sophistication.
   d. Automatic recorders can be used to prerecord the presenta-
      tion and automatically change the slides.
   e. Slides tend to give you an outline for a talk. They can be
      used for notes with the presentation.
2. Guidelines:
   a. Be sure that you have planned your presentation to give
      adequate time to each slide. It is hard to show more than
      two or three slides per minute.
   b. Try out the slide projector and screen ahead of time to
      make sure everyone in the room can see the images. Check
      the lighting.
   c. Have an extra bulb available.
   d. Number the slides in case you drop them.
   e. Check the slides just before the presentation to make sure
      they are all in the carousel right side up.

      f. Use a remote slide changer or have someone else change the slides to you can stay at the front of the room.

3. Disadvantages:
    a. Slides must be shown in a dark room. This allows people to drift off or even sleep. After lunch is not a good time for slides. And if the room can't be darkened, the slides won't show up well.
    b. Slides take the focus off the presenter.
    c. Slides cannot be changed at the last minute, like flip charts and overheads.

Now about participation. Your presentation certainly allows for some give and take, questions from the prospect. But can you plan their participation? To some extent you can. And you can at least try to anticipate the kinds of questions or interaction you might have. You also can encourage it. Now, I'm aware that by the time you have gotten to this point with your prospect there has been a lot of interaction. You have asked questions and listened for problems, goals, and so on. The prospect is used to having you listen to his input, even take notes. But I find that a lot of professionals forget all about this when it comes time for the presentation. It is as if we lose our authority if anyone butts in. Nothing could be further from the truth.

However, the interaction has to be managed. First, look back over your audience analysis. Which people are apt to ask questions or make comments? What will they ask? What do you want them to ask or say? Put all down this in writing.

You can encourage participation in several ways but the easiest is to ask questions at strategic points during the presentation. Plan these out ahead of time.

Then there are those questions that come up that you didn't anticipate or want. You can continue to control the presentation by simply saying, "I want to answer that question for you, but first let me..." There is no rule that says you have to answer a question the minute it is asked. Make a strong mental note of the question so you can come back to it later. If you are working with a flip chart you can even write it down in abbreviated form.

As you develop your presentation pay attention to the style of those in the audience. If you have used the forms above you have a general idea of the style of each of the members of the audience. Now ask yourself, "Who is the decision maker?" "What is his/her style?" "Who are the influencers and what are their styles?"

You then need to gear your presentation to match the style of those you most want to influence. The following is a very limited guide to presenting to each of the styles:

The Driver: makes decisions based on facts and usually just hits the highlights. The driver will look at enough of the details to be satisfied that the facts are accurate. The driver is influenced by tangible results. He will often go right to the fee section of the proposal. He may interrupt your verbal presentation to get to the bottom line quicker. The driver wants fast action.

The Expressive: will make a fast decision based on people, how he will look, his role in the solution, and so on. Details bore him. He will be interested in a good "feel" for the people who will be involved in the project.

The Amiable: is interested in relationships and maintaining the status quo. Showing him how the new proposal will solve the problem in much the same way that past solutions have been found will be helpful. The amiable is more comfortable with others being in on the decision and giving support to it. If the amiable is the decision maker, then the influencers will probably play a larger role.

The Analytical: needs to be right. He will check the details of the proposal to feel comfortable with the process. Details of the process are important to the analytical. Though it is important to stress the benefits of your solution rather than the features, the analytical is also interested in the features. If there is a physical or manufacturing process involved in your product or service, invite the analytical to your plant to see the process work.

Here is a generic proposal for one of my services presented in outline form. The proposal is for a general training program to convert the bank to a sales culture.

The driver will check the roman numeral headings, check out one or two details, then turn to the fee page.

The expressive will glance through the proposal and ask you to tell him about it.

The amiable will study the proposal and show it to associates to get their opinions and feelings about it.

PROPOSAL

Based on my understanding of your situation and objectives as outlined above, the following is a discussion draft of ways in which Kendall Marketing might be of help in achieving these goals:

I. Needs assessment:

  A. Purposes:

   1. To gain a clear understanding of the situation within the Bank and in the marketplace.
   2. To develop input for the type of sales program and training needed from those who will make it work.
   3. To gain ownership in the resultant program on the part of all involved.

  B. Method:

   1. Kendall will interview some fifteen to eighteen of the Bank's officers and employees with a good representation of all levels, all departments, and all locations.
   2. The interviews will take forty-five minutes to one hour and will be completely confidential. Management will only receive a synopsis of the results, no individual comments.
   3. The interviews will follow a structured outline but the face-to-face format will allow for probing and clarification where indicated.
   4. Kendall will also take a thorough drive through the territory to supplement the survey done during the initial visit.
   5. Kendall will study the report by the opinion-research firm hired earlier.

  C. Management will receive a report which will include:

   1. A question-by-question synopsis of the interviews.

      2. Significant findings from the interviews and the drive of the territory.

      3. Recommendations for needed changes in the marketing program, needed services, and training needs at all levels.

II. Sales systems:

  A. New accounts cross-selling:

      1. Kendall will work with _____ and others to develop a workable system for tracking, encouraging, and rewarding cross-selling at the new accounts desks.

      2. Based on findings in the needs assessment above, the system may include on-desk sales systems, cross-sell index tracking, and incentive programs.

  B. Kendall will work with _____ and others to set up a sales referral systems for all lobby personnel.

  C. Kendall will work with _____ to develop a maximum officer call system that may include tracking and reporting systems for sales management, quotas, and incentives.

III. New products and pricing:

  A. Kendall will work with _____ in the selection and outlining of new products as needed from the study above.

  B. Kendall will review the pricing of all services and work with the marketing coordinator in the development of a pricing strategy that will fit all branch markets.

IV. Training: Based on findings in the interview process and studies above, the training will possibly consist of:

  A. Officer call training:

      1. Initial training will probably follow the attached outline.

      2. Videotaped role plays will be handled on a two-at-a-time basis.

3. A continuing-training schedule will be set up with the marketing coordinator for subsequent marketing meetings.

B. New accounts training will probably consist of some combination of:

1. Understanding people, dealing with irate customers, etc.
2. The sales process, how it works.
3. A system of questions to be asked of all customers.
4. Perhaps a flip chart for the desk and a sales system for all services.

C. The training for the remainder of the staff will probably consist of some combination of:

1. Understanding people, dealing with irate customers, etc.
2. Standards for greeting every customer, whether face-to-face or on the phone.
3. Listening for sales opportunities and what to do with them.

D. Some staff member should be trained in how to continue some of this training for new hires and review.

V. Fees:

A. For the entire program I through IV above: $11,500.00

B. Payment schedule

1. With contract $4,000.00
2. Following first report $2,000.00
3. Monthly progress payments based on amount of work completed.

C. There will be a $25 per person charge for each officer trainee. This training will include a notebook, self-assessment instrument and videotaped audiovisual support.

D. All fees are in addition to travel and out-of-pocket expenses.

E. The client is responsible for the cost of printing of
material for all training except the officer call training. The client is also responsible for any sales systems, computer software, or hardware that the client
decides to use in the sales process. Any costs of
training, such as off-premise training rooms, travel,
food, breaks, audiovisual equipment, etc., will also be
borne by the client.

The analytical will go over the details, maybe several times, and
test out all of the hypotheses in his mind, if not in actual trials.
Give him time to do that. Guarantees included in the proposal are
also attractive to the analytical.

These are guidelines, of course. Whenever you try to put people
in a box and predict their behavior you are asking for trouble. But it
is reasonable to expect some of this behavior, especially if your
prospect is clearly in a corner on the style model.

The outline format, then, has something for everyone. It directs
the faster moving drivers and expressives to the key points and yet
gives the slower movers the detail they need to feel comfortable
with their decision. If you have a situation in which several people
are apt to read your proposal and you don't know their style, then an
outline format can be effective.

By now you have asked questions, listened, and found the
problem. You've given a Summary Feedback to clarify misunder-
standings and show that you have listened and care. You have made
a presentation of your solution. It is time to ask for the business.
This one scares a lot of people so I've devoted a whole chapter to
this rather small but critical part of the sales process.

11

What's Our Next Step?

MY nephew is in his early twenties and single. He told me about a girl he met whom he found very attractive. He was talking to her about an article he wrote in the campus newspaper.

"Yes. I read it. I thought it was fascinating. Have you written any others?" He admitted that he had. "I'd love to read the others," she said.

When he told me about the conversation, I said, "Blake, we call that a buying signal when we're out making sales calls. It may be time to ask for the business."

People usually tell us when they are ready to buy. They give us signals. They ask questions like, "If we did this, when could you get around to starting the project?" That is called a buying signal. Almost any statement or question that places the prospect in the solution is a buying signal. When I make calls with people who are new to selling, I often see them miss the buying signals.

Buying signals can take many forms. They will differ based on the circumstances, the product, the prospect. You will have to learn to listen for the ones that match your situation. However, here are a few you might recognize.

"I'm not sure I can afford the solution (product, service, etc.)." This a really a question of value. Will I get my problem solved in a cost-effective manner? Will it pay me back as much as I have to spend?

For this one I ask a question to get the prospect involved in the solution. I might ask, "How much more money do you think you can make (or how much do you think you can save) if we solve your problem?" Based on the answer I can then couch my pricing in terms of the payback. "The cost of our service is less than 20 percent of that amount. Does that sound interesting to you?"

137

Another buying signal might be the asking of questions about how the solution will work and how the prospect will be affected. Questions like "Will the installation disrupt our offices for very long" indicate that the prospect is beginning to picture himself in the solution, in *your* solution.

Asking for references is another sure buying signal. I usually include a list of references in any written proposal. I try to relate the references to the type of prospect I'm dealing with, those with similar problems. It is all right to tell the prospect that you will put together a list and fax it to him. Give yourself time to think. But keep in mind that this is a buying signal. Time is of the essence.

If you have done much selling you know the concept of buying signals. You may not have called it that but you recognize the feeling. At any rate, once you grasp the concept you will be able to recognize those buying signals that pertain to your business. Then a decision has to be made. Are the buying signals strong enough that the prospect is ready to buy? Is it time to ask about the buying decision? I can't tell you exactly when that time has come. You will have to feel your way along by trial and error. Perhaps you already have a feel for this.

Timing is critical in asking for the business. Sometimes if you ask too soon you get a no that is hard to overcome later on. There is indeed an art to the timing. However, making a mistake is part of the learning process. At times I might even include the prospect in that process. I may ask, "I tried to make the sale too soon, didn't I?" and see what he says. If you've lost the sale anyway you don't have much to lose and this show of honesty might even make a friend.

So now it is time to ask for the business. If you are typical of many of the professional people I work with, the very thought of this strikes terror into your soul. Well, maybe that is a bit dramatic, but there is a fear factor. We need to look at that fear realistically.

In much of the sales training I have seen the instructor will call this part of the selling process the "close." I hate that word. It sounds so manipulative. I heard a real estate salesman talking to a group of bankers once and he said, "The old adage in real estate is 'location, location, location.' Well, in sales the byword is 'close, close, close.'" I could almost feel the revulsion in the room. I could certainly feel it in my own gut.

The term *close* may have come from the old days of pots and pan salespeople going door to door. They would try to get the money and then "close" the door so they could get to the bank and clear the check. In my business and in many I work with the sale is actually an opening of a relationship, a beginning, not a close. Even in a situation where the sales staff makes the sale and turns the prospect over to another department for the execution, that salesperson is still involved with the client. It would seem better to call this step the "opening" rather than the "close." So much for my prejudices.

Let's talk about the fear. If you don't have any fear in asking for the business, skip this part. This is for my sensitive friends who are like me. This part scares me to death. What if they say "No"? They have rejected me personally. I hate that.

Early in my career as a consultant I called on an old friend, a former colleague from my Allied Bancshares days. He was then the president of the his own bank, a bank that fit my profile of prospects. His name was Roy Joe. Only in Texas can a man with a name like Roy Joe become president of a bank. Roy was an excellent marketing banker, one of the few. We talked about his bank. I asked questions. Where was he headed? What problems did he have? I asked every question I could think of to ferret out any problem for which I had a solution. He had a call program. He was doing training. He showed me his written marketing plan. It was good.

Finally, I wrapped up by saying, "Roy Joe, I've asked you every question in the book about marketing. You've had a good answer for every one of them. I really don't think you need me." Those were my actual words. I was honest in my feelings.

Roy said, "Dick, if I ever hire a marketing consultant you will be the one. I've known you for years and I know your work. You're good. But I agree with you. We are in pretty good shape where marketing is concerned. I don't think we need you."

I left the bank and drove back to my office. A sick feeling came up in the pit of my stomach. I had been rejected. I had been rejected by an old friend. I was a little kid being told I couldn't play in my neighbor's sandbox. I was unwanted, unfit. I had even told Roy to reject me. I had been the instigator. I was the judge. Still I felt the rejection. As a grown man I hate to admit these seemingly childish feelings. But they are real and they affect my decision to ask for the business next time. I have to admit I have them and look them square in the eye.

You may not have such strong feelings or you may feel worse. I wish I had a quick fix to prevent these feelings but I don't. I do have a few ideas about how to avoid setting yourself up for the rejection.

When these feelings of rejection come over me it helps if I reassure myself that it is not me that is being rejected. At worst the prospect is rejecting my service, product, or company. Probably, he is really dealing with his own fear of change and therefore saying no to anything new. It may have little if anything to do with me. After the pain of the feelings subsides I will have plenty of time to evaluate how I might have done a better job of helping the prospect through that fear. For now I need to learn to not take it personally.

I have a magic phrase to help avoid rejection: "Mr. Prospect, what is our next step?" Instead of asking outright for the business with a question like, "Mr. Prospect, what's it going to take to get your business?" I take the softer approach. I put the ball back in the prospect's court. His answer, then, will not be a rejection. It may well be, "How do I sign up?" Or "What does your calendar look like the first of next month? Can you start then?"

Or it may be, "Let me think about it. Call me next week." You are still in the process. You are not rejected. It may be, "I just don't think this is quite what we need right now. I guess the next step is to keep looking." This is an opportunity to reopen the questioning. You might say, "I understand your feelings. There are some other people at our shop who may have some ideas on your situation. Would you mind if I go over my notes with them and get back to you if I find a different approach?"

For what it's worth, I almost never ask outright for someone to buy. I have found over the years that if I have done my work well in the sales interview, the question about the next step is all it takes.

I may review the sales interview. "Mr. Prospect, let me review where I think we are. Do you think we have a pretty good feel for your situation, your goals, the problems that you are facing?" I wait for an answer. If it is positive I continue. "You've shown a lot of interest in my telling you about how we've solved similar problems for other companies like yours. If you think I've covered everything, what do you think our next step ought to be?"

This question relieves the pressure from both of us. The prospect can feel open to exploring possibilities without having to think only in terms of buy or don't buy. It also continues the consultative relationship. We are a team looking for a solution. It is nonadversarial.

In their national bestselling book on negotiations, *Getting to Yes*, Roger Fisher and William Ury give three criteria for successful negotiation. (Selling is one form of negotiation.) They state, "Any method of negotiation may be fairly judged by these criteria: It should be a wise agreement if agreement is possible. It should be efficient. *And it should improve or at least not damage the relationship between the parties.* (Italics are mine.)

Not long ago I had made a sales call on a bank in another city. The prospect banker asked if he could send two of the bank officers to visit one of my client referrals. I set up the meeting. The two prospect bankers flew in the night before and I took them to dinner. I helped them organize their questioning for the next day. The client banker was kind enough to spend two or three hours with them going over all the details of how our consulting process worked in his specific situation. I remember hearing him say, "I only wish we had gotten Dick in here a few months earlier."

As we parted at the airport and headed to our respective planes I asked, "What else do you need for me to do?" I did *not* ask for the business. I maintained the role of consultant. Here was their answer: "Dick, I think it's up to us now. We have a meeting of the management committee next Thursday. I'm going to recommend we hire you. Call me Friday and I should have an answer." I did and they did, and they are now a good client.

Every company has its own buying style. In your planning stage you need to try to figure out what it is and prepare your presentation and the asking for the business to accommodate that.

More and more these days you will find companies using committees to make buying decisions. This increases the difficulty of the planning process. You need to know who the decision maker is. Is it the committee? Does the committee report to a higher level with recommendations? If so, is your proposal geared to the committee *and* the decision maker? Many times you won't be able to tell. Therefore your proposal has to address the fears of all four styles.

Have you determined the committee's style? Most committees have a style similar to the individual style. What is that style? Does your proposal address that style? Sometimes you can just ask who the decision maker is and what that style might be. Other times the committee will feel that you are going over their heads. This takes a gut feel. Experience is the best teacher. There are times after I fail to make a sale that I call back and ask why. I tell the prospect that this is to help my marketing in the future. Most people will cooperate with this kind of effort. The answers will probably give you ideas for the next proposal. At any rate the questioning expands the relationship and may be of value in the future with this same prospect. People like to help. It makes them feel a part of your organization, a good relationship-building exercise.

At other times you are talking to the decision maker. Sometimes that is obvious. At other times it is not. A question like "If you decide to go with us on this, how will the decision actually be made?" can sometimes give you the answer.

The builder's supply house I talked about earlier was a small company bought by an ex-banker. He had seven employees. He had discussed their concerns about their jobs when he took over the operations. This told me that he was the decision maker and would not consult them about the purchase.

Take the case of the architectural firm working with the church committee for the construction of the conference center. The architects were dealing with a committee that would make a recommendation to a still larger committee or board. This one is more difficult but fairly typical in many cases. In this case the presentation has to be put together so that the committee is armed for the presentation to the larger group. It is almost a train-the-trainer situation. A slide presentation that presents itself is one way to get around this problem.

Of course, a face-to-face encounter with the decision maker is ideal. It never hurts to ask for this if the first interviewee(s) seems agreeable. Many times the initial interviewee has been assigned the task of making the recommendation and would welcome the support to take the pressure off him.

If you feel a high comfort level with the initial interviewee you might ask further questions to determine what the decision maker might need. You can put yourself in the role of a partner with the interviewee helping him do his job, making him look good to his boss. The same is true for committees. You actually are going through the interviewing process with the decision maker in the third person.

There are almost as many buying styles as there are companies that use them. Another style is the hierarchy of decision levels. Many banks have levels of loan limits. Bankers are actually "buying" your request for a loan. The loan officer you are talking to may have one limit. He can double this limit by getting another peer to sign the loan request. His boss has a higher limit and can approve a loan up to that limit for your officer. Loans above that limit have to go the loan committee. Many companies structure their purchasing limits in a similar manner. Knowing what these limits are is extremely helpful both in the presentation and in the pricing of your product or service.

Remember the styles of those with whom you are dealing. With the driver be prepared for quick factual answers to any questions. Be direct. Have the highlights of the proposal easily accessible. Show tangible results.

With the expressive also be quick with the answers. Show how the proposal will make the expressive look good. Be sensitive about going over his head. Play the role of his being the decision maker even if you suspect he is not.

With the amiable stress relationships, how your proposal will help him build his relationship with others in the company. Stress the importance of your relationship with him. Offering to go to the decision maker with your presentation is probably more acceptable here. Show concern for his feelings. Using third-party stories with people he knows is helpful.

With the analytical be prepared with detail about how the proposal will work to solve the problems. The analytical may also want to know about how the process of your solution works. He will want to picture all of the actual workings of the process. Where will he fit in? What kinds of problems might he encounter? How will you solve them? The analytical has trained himself to think of everything that can go wrong so that he will have an answer to it. Help him be prepared. Assure him that you, too, have thought of and dealt with these problems in the past. Guarantees are often effective with the analytical.

To some extent the same rules apply with the style of the committee or the company as a whole. Keep all of this in mind when planning your proposal and asking for the business.

When asking for the business, a bolder approach is often effective with the driver. A question like, "What will it take for us to get the business?" is more acceptable with a driver. You may feel uncomfortable with it. But remember: We are willing to be uncomfortable to make our prospect comfortable. Again, experience is the best teacher. Try some different approaches. Learn from your mistakes.

Objections. Another word that strikes fear into the heart of many a salesperson. I have been to so many sales seminars where the instructor promises "twenty-seven ways to overcome objections" that I'm tempted not to talk about them. They are a reality, however, and so we must deal with them.

Some people say that objections are an opportunity to sell. I think they are a problem. I don't like them. I want the prospect to see the wisdom of my presentation and accept my proposal. But that is not always the case and hence I have to deal with objections. I do that in a manner similar to the entire sales process.

First, I repeat the objection in my own words to make sure I have understood it.

"The price is too high."

"Let me make sure I've understood what you are saying. You like my proposal, think it might solve your problem, but you don't have the budget. Is that about it?"

This lets the prospect know I've heard him. It shows my concern. It shows I'm not defensive. It lets him hear my phrasing of the objection. It may open the way for him to clarify his objection.

"Well, it's not really a budget problem. It's just that I've been talking to other consultants and I think I can do the same thing for less money." Now I have something to work with. He has introduced the idea of my competition. I now feel free to ask about them. Who are they? What have they proposed? We are still looking for value with a cost/benefit equation.

Often, after I have gotten agreement on what the objection really is, I ask for clarification. "If you like the proposal and think it would solve your problem, what do you think would be a fair price?" I'm opening a dialogue that will let me in on the decision-making process.

Or I might ask, "What particularly about the proposal do you think is out of line?" Here I am asking for specifics, again so that I can have a dialogue about the decision-making process.

The objection might be, "I don't think we have the man power to get us through the changes you are proposing."

My response, "You feel that our proposed changes will take a lot of man power?"

"Yes. It sounds like that to me."

"How much man power do you feel it will take?" And we're off discussing details about how the prospect wants the problem solved. It may well be that I have to rewrite the proposal. I might have misunderstood some aspect of the prospect's problem.

In general, objections are obstacles. But they do happen. I need to think of them in the same way that I think of the initial interview. They are giving me information about a problem on which I can base a proposed solution.

I need to keep in mind, too, that the objection may well be a valid reason for declining my proposal. In this case, using these probing mechanisms I can side with my prospect and assure him that I agree that I'm not the one for the job. I might even help him find the right party. The worst this will do for me is make a friend. Who knows? I may get the next job, which is even bigger and better.

In the way of wrap-up, if you have done your work well in asking questions, listening, helping to uncover problems, giving feedback to show that you understand and care, getting the business may take care of itself. At any rate, this part of the sales process can be somewhat frightening. Remember the words of John Cassis: "Step into your fear. That will give you power."

12

Gee, I Hate Paperwork

Y OU have made a call. You have made a sale. You have not made a sale. You have made the first call in what promises to be a series leading to a sale. It doesn't matter. Follow-up is required for any of the above—and this is where a lot of people in sales fall down on the job. Here is where *I* fall down on the job. I can teach this stuff a whole lot better than I do it.

Let's take the situation in which you have made a call but not a sale. You have discovered some problems that may lead to a sale down the road. It is just the first call. You have gotten acquainted. What do you do?

You write a letter. If it is appropriate, include a summary of your notes. The letter might look something like the one that appears on page 147.

By the way, some people think you shouldn't thank people for their time. They feel that it is suggesting that your time is not as valuable as the prospect's. I personally prefer the more humble approach of thanking them. It's a matter of choice, though.

After writing the letter you need to send a copy to John Floyd along with a copy of your notes (whether or not you included them in the letter). This will alert John to the call and make him aware of the results of the call and your expectations for the next call along with the time frame.

Next you need to make a copy in your records of the call and set up your tickler for the next call. That brings up your record keeping. There are some wonderful software packages on the market today to help you with this. I use ACT!™ myself, but there are several other brands.

Mr. Joe Prospect
President
XYZ Corporation
123 Any Street
Any City, USA

Dear Joe:

It was great to have a visit with you today. I thank you for taking the time to see me.

It was good to get to know you and a little about your company. I have summarized my notes and have included a copy of what will go in my file about XYZ Corporation. You might look it over to make sure I have a clear picture of your situation. Let me know if I need to make any corrections.

In general, I was quite impressed with what I saw in your operations. Your marketing program seems well thought out and is working pretty well. I did take note of the fact that you are a little concerned about the effectiveness of your outside sales team. According to the data you showed me your salespeople seem to be doing a little below the average for your industry. Perhaps we can discuss this at our next meeting. I have some ideas I would like to get your reaction to.

I hope you and your wife have a great time on your cruise to the Caribbean next month. I know you'll be pretty busy until after you get back. I will call you after you've had time to uncover your desk after the trip. I'd like to bring John Floyd by to meet you.

Thanks again for taking the time to see me.

Sincerely,

Dick Kendall
President

DK/ps

Here are some things a software package should do for you:

Record of clients and prospects:
1. Give you a list of prospects and clients.
2. Record basic information about the companies, including address, phone, key people, titles, etc.
3. Keep a record of other information pertinent to your business, which might include sales, number of employees, type of industry (SIC codes), and other items you need.
4. Show a call record by company, who called on whom, when, the results, and the callback date.

Records of calls made:
1. Show who was called on at which company.
2. Who made the call, including any joint calls.
3. Give the date of the call.
4. Show what happened of any significance (a problem was found).
5. Show the callback date if any.

If I make a call on a company I want to see a complete review of the calling history prior to my call.

A foolproof tickler system:
1. Show the date and time for a callback.
2. Whether the callback should be phone, person, fax, or mail.
3. Who should make the call.
4. The purpose of the callback.
5. Give adequate warning that the callback time is approaching.

Some other features provided by most software:
1. Many customizable fields.
2. Space for home phones and personalized information about the client/prospect.
3. Search systems that allow you to select a group of prospects or clients by type of business, size of business, prospect or client, called on in a time frame, done business with in a time frame, etc. Some of my clients record hobbies like golf. Then they search up the group of golfers for a golf tournament.

4. Dialing features that dial the number for you through your modem, record the length of the call, the purpose of the call, and the follow-up or disposition.
5. A word processor that allows you to automatically send follow-up letters, faxes, etc.
6. Many more features you may never use.

It may be that you are managing others in a calling effort. If so you need reports on each of their calling records. The following are minimal reports that you need in order to manage their calling activity. These same reports are helpful if you are only monitoring your own calling efforts. The reports will have to be timed to match your calling activity. If you make eight or ten calls a week you should print out the report weekly. If you make eight or ten calls a month then print the report monthly, etc.

Report of Calls for Joe Smith
For the week of November 10–14, 1996

XYZ Corporation   **Callback date**
John Doe, President   May 15, 1997
November 10, 1996   **Time:** 10:00 a.m.
Results: He is considering buying property next door to expand his warehouse space. May need a loan for purchase of the land. May lead to a mortgage on the building.
Purpose of the callback: follow-up on the loan possibilities.
Who to call: Take Bill Roberts with me.   Type of call: Person

Jones and Associates   **Callback date**
Bob Jones, President   March 24, 1997
November 10, 1996   **Time:** 2:00 p.m.
Results: He is expanding his staff to include two more trainers. May need a working capital loan. Will know more after the first of the year.
Purpose of the callback: To get an update on his progress, discuss loan possibilities, check out collateral.
Who to call: Me.   Type of call: Person

Robert's Pharmaceuticals   **Callback date**
Jim Roberts, President   June 15, 1996
November 1, 1996   **Time:** 0:00
Results: He borrows money from time to time to expand
inventory. Has a mortgage on the property with First State Bank.
Could be a prospect for a revolving line of credit.
Purpose of the callback: Just to stay in touch, look for problems.
Who to call: Me.   Type of call: Person

Cruz Machine Works   **Callback date**
Ron Cruz, Owner   January 15, 1997
November 12, 1996   **Time:** 0:00
Results: He has placed a bid for a manufacturing process to a
major supplier of oil-field equipment. Will know if he won the bid
after the first of the year. Will need significant financing for
supplies, inventory, and accounts receivable.
Purpose of the callback: To check on the success of the bid and
discuss a financing package.
Who to call: Take Bob Ables to flesh out details of the accounts
receivable financing.   Type of call: Person

This should be enough to give you the idea. If you are managing
others this gives you enough information to evaluate the
effectiveness of the calls, see if you need to be involved in the next
call and manage the ongoing calling process.

If you are only managing your own calling this will give you a
management tool to measure your own effectiveness. Maintaining
these records gives you a calling history. Later you can check back
and measure your results against efforts.

These examples, obviously, are for bankers. You will need to
make changes in the content to match your own business needs.

Obviously, the computer program cannot do much in the way of
input into the program. Each salesperson will have to be trained in
filling out the reports to get the right results.

Although this discussion has assumed the use of a computer, the
same information can be kept manually if the calling volume is low.
However, if you have a computer the software is pretty inexpensive.

If you are managing several people who are making sales then you might also want a summary of call and sales information. A form like this can be adapted to your specific needs.

NAME	NUMBER OF CALLS				SALES	
	Phone		Person			
	Cust.	Pros.	Cust.	Pros.	Widgets	Baubles
Joe Jones	6	8	2	4	28,000	14,900
Don Thomas	2	1	0	3	14,000	10,200
John Floyd	1	8	1	6	24,000	18,000
James Brown	19	1	7	1	15,000	12,000
Bill Abrams	2	8	1	1	10,000	18,000
Gary Carson	8	2	9	2	27,000	26,000

You can make this form for the current period, be that a week, a month, a quarter. Then you can add another form that gives the same information for year-to-date. This form is particularly useful when several people in management will be seeing it. In small banks that I work with I have this form distributed to the board of directors. It gives the calling officers recognition for their efforts and also lets them know that their efforts are being monitored at the top. This, of course, depends on the structure of the organization and its management style.

Back to the individual's record keeping on each prospect. If you have taken good notes you need to save them. Write them up in an organized fashion. This takes discipline. It gets easier after a few tries. This will be of great help later on when you need them for a second call. Often these can be sent to the client. They are invaluable when you are getting ready to make a proposal.

Sometimes it is appropriate to send them to the client in your follow-up letter, sometimes not. At any rate they are good for the files. This assumes, then, that you will make a file on every prospect. You may not. If you make a lot of calls you may just keep them all in one file, provided you can find them and make use of them in the future.

Copies of the notes should be sent to anyone else in your organization that might later be affected by this prospect. By all means send them to the other person that you have designated to make a follow-up call. Alert that person to the call and the timing so that they can set up a tickler in their record-keeping system.

There is a lot more to do in the way of follow-up. People forget. Even if you have made a good impression on someone their memory will fade over time. They may get to a point where the problem you have discussed with them becomes more important to them. You want them to remember you. The following suggestions might be helpful.

I knew one fellow who would carry postcards with him when he traveled. He made a point of writing five post cards a day to ongoing prospects. He would keep a list of his call records with him. He would make a note about the person's problem and some idea that had come to mind about it. Or he would quote an article. Sometimes he would send a copy of the article that applied.

I mentioned earlier the banker who would send copies of our bank's quarterly statement to each one of his prospects. He would make a personalized note to each one of them mentioning his visit if at all appropriate. He would renew the conversation about any problems they had discussed. This took him several hours but he set that time aside every quarter.

Some companies send out newsletters. These are fairly easy to fill. One of my clients reads all of the trade magazines for his industry. As he reads he highlights items of interest in each article. When he writes his newsletter much of it is filled with bullet items that he has lifted from the magazines. This saves his prospects and clients reading time and makes them look forward to getting the newsletter. He then adds a problem/solution story from his own client experiences. He has a short blurb about his company services in a box in the newsletter. He leaves space in the header or the margins to write personal notes when appropriate.

One of the really effective uses for the newsletter is in networking. He always carries several copies of his newsletter in his coat pocket. When he meets someone at a business or some social situations the conversation nearly always gets around to, "What do you do?" During the conversation my friend produces a copy of the newsletter and gives it to his new acquaintance.

"This will give you some idea of our business. We put that out quarterly. I'd be happy to put you on our mailing list if you'd be interested." Then he has a new prospect. At one time he hand-delivered specially silk-screened three-ring binders with his company's name, address, and phone number on it. The newsletters were three hole punched and many of his prospects and clients would save the newsletters in that binder. It is really comforting when you are making a first call on someone to see a binder on their desk with your company name on it. It's a natural ice breaker.

I read a national study that showed it takes an average of five calls to make a sale. Follow-up is essential if you are going to ever make a sale. This is particularly true if you are in a relationship-type business where you depend on long-term, repeat sales.

I jokingly tell bankers, "If you go make a cold call on a prospect and he agrees to move all of his banking business over to your bank on that same day—check his credit." There is something wrong with someone who is that anxious to find a new bank. It has been my experience that to some extent the same is true of many businesses. People are slow to let go of suppliers and service companies with whom they have had long-term relationships. This seems to be true even when the relationship is not serving them well.

But let's assume you have made a sale. How about follow-up there? Critical. Often this vital part of the sale is left undone or done half-way. Now is the time to cement the relationship we have opened.

You will want to write a letter. However, in the letter you will want to tell the new customer about what you have done to set up his account. So let's look at that first.

You have a system for setting up a new customer. If you are in a company of any size this may involve other departments or other people. This is a good place to use the Summary Feedback instrument. Make copies of it for all those who will be involved with the customer.

You may have to get credit established. If so, take care of that. Credit people love the Summary Feedback. You may have to be a go-between in getting necessary information.

Who else will be involved? Will the actual service be administered by another person? Get them involved. Give them a copy of the Summary Feedback. Discuss how the new client will be handled. This person will need to know what you have offered, what you have promised in providing the product or service.

This is a good place for lunch. As I have said, I don't like lunches for sales calls. It's hard to take notes. It is hard to keep the conversation focused. But here you are expanding your relationship with others in the company. The relaxed atmosphere of a restaurant can help this process.

So now the letter (See page 155).

After writing the letter I mark my calendar for Monday to set up the lunch date. I also make sure that any other details that are my responsibility are on the calendar. In addition I mark my calendar for appropriate dates to double-check with John Floyd, the credit department, and others to see that they have done everything I said they would. My word is on the line. The new client is still considering me the primary relationship until the work is under way.

Then I mark my calendar for a couple weeks after our lunch to play "black hat/white hat" with the client. I call him and say, "Joe, I've turned you over to John Floyd. He's the best man in our company for your type of work. In fact, he's one of the best in the business. But I still feel responsible for our relationship with you. How's it going? Is John doing everything I said he would? Are you pleased with the way our company is treating you?" Then I listen.

I keep a relationship with John Floyd so that he knows I'm playing this role. Therefore, if there are any problems I go straight to John and we work them out. If all is going well I tell John and reinforce the relationship there.

Keeping a good account is a whole lot easier than getting a new one. You've been successful in business so you probably already do this kind of thing. But it never hurts to be reminded. Congratulations! You've locked in another long-term, loyal customer relationship.

Mr. Joe Customer
President
XYZ Corporation
123 Any Street
Any City, USA
Dear Joe:

I wanted to put into writing my elation at being able to welcome you to our fine family of clients. I look forward to a long and productive relationship with you and XYZ Corporation.

The ball has already started rolling at our end. I took your annual report to our credit department. Susan Morrow will be contacting you in the next couple of days for additional information. Let me know if there is anything I can do to smooth that process for you.

As we discussed, John Floyd will be the primary manager for your account. Even though you met him on our second visit I think it would be good for all three of us to have lunch together soon so that he can meet his contact at your company. I'll call you next Monday to set that up.

I have shared my background summary on your company with several of the staff. They are looking forward to meeting you at some time in the future.

Joe, even though John will be your primary account manager, I want you to know that I take our relationship personally and will continue to stay in touch. Also please let me know if there is anything I can do to help make the transition to our firm as effortless as possible.

Thank you.
Sincerely,

Dick Kendall

13

Clients Are Where You Find Them

WE'VE covered the sales call in great detail. We've talked about the introduction and developing rapport. We've discussed a Call Purpose Statement and the development of problems. We've given a Summary Feedback, presented a solution, and actually gotten the business. Then we followed up after the call and the sale.

You may now be thinking, "That's great but where do I get to practice all I've learned? How do I know who to call on? And once I have decided that, how do I get ready to make the call?"

Part of the answer to these questions is called "prospecting," finding prospects that might be interested in our product or services, the people who have the problems we can solve. The other part is called "research," getting ready to make the call.

Prospecting is an unending job. As long as we are in business to help people solve problems then the search for those who have problems is ongoing.

You may be in a large corporation that has a marketing department that does the prospecting job for you. In that case you may want to skip to the part about research later in this chapter. However, before you go, let me tell you that it is my belief that everyone in every organization has a responsibility for prospecting. Without prospects we have no company. Without the company we have no job.

I do some training for a major oil company. One of my students was a research assistant in the company's lab, which tested their gasoline as well as that of their competitors. I was talking to him about my always buying the gasoline of the company we both worked for. He said, "I never do. Brand X is better. We've tested it."

I think that fellow should be taken out and shot. Not really. But I do think he should try to go to work for Brand X. Life is too short for me to work for a company whose products I don't believe in. If you feel the same way then you want your company to succeed. If your company succeeds then it must have new prospects for its goods and services. And that is where you come in.

Everyone who works for a company can be the eyes and ears of the marketing department. Every contact, every friend, every fellow club member, and so on can be a potential client for my company. A company with 100 employees and a two-person marketing department can have 100 pairs of eyes and ears, 100 relationship builders, 100 prospectors. So maybe you want to read this section after all.

At this point you may be thinking that I am asking you to take advantage of your friends. I am. But let's put that in a different context. You are in business to solve problems for your clients or customers. Do you *not* want to solve the problems of a friend because he or she is a friend?

Years ago, in my callow youth when I was marketing director for that little bank in Conroe, I learned a number of valuable lessons. One of them had to do with my relationship to friends in business.

When the group out of Houston bought the bank they put Willie Whitehead (his real name) in as president. Actually Willie was one of the owners. Willie brought a charming country touch to banking. Willie was from outside of Carlyle, Texas, which is outside of Groveton, which is outside of Lufkin, which is outside of nowhere. Willie came by his country ways honestly. Even with his expensive suits and impeccable taste in clothes the country shined through. It was part of his endearing charm.

Willie didn't have much college but he made up for that in self-education. He was one of the smartest men I have known. He knew more about banking than most Harvard MBAs could hope to learn in a lifetime. I learned a lot from Willie.

Shortly after the bank was sold and Willie became my boss, my wife and I were out at the country club for dinner. We ran into some old friends. They joined us. After dinner I magnanimously signed all of our dinners to my membership, which actually was a bank membership.

The next day I was talking to Willie and told him about the dinner. I said, "I feel funny putting that on my expense account since these are old friends."

Then Willie gave me one of his many gems, "Dick, we don't want to penalize people because they happen to be our friends."

Aristotle distinguished three kinds of friendship. The first is friendship based on utility, as when businessmen cultivate one another in hopes of improving their businesses; second is friendship based on pleasure, as when we attend a party in a social setting. The third is what Aristotle calls perfect friendship, based on the admiration of the character of the other person. Though Aristotle said the third is precious, he also said it is rare. And note that he did not say that the other two are bad; they are quite necessary.

Do I want my friends to do business with me? Of course I do. But I feel reluctant to ask them. Maybe you do, too. Part of that reluctance has to do with what has been lovingly called my "fraud complex." A fraud complex is the belief that you are really no good and given enough time people will find it out. Friends being long-term contacts will be sure to find out if we do work for them. So don't. Or do it free. I hope you don't have this problem but I thought you might find it interesting that I do—and I wrote the book.

I have a friend who sells equipment to a specialized group of manufacturing concerns. I know I could help him sell more with a carefully thought out marketing plan. He could move from making a good living to getting a really good business going. I've talked to him about it but I've also listened to his side. Part of what I hear in his approach to business is that he doesn't want to get a "good" business going. He is happy where he is. He's not doing all the marketing he knows how to do now. He just doesn't want to. Like many of my prospects, the commitment to change is greater than the commitment to my fee. I have left it alone.

There is an old story from the 1930s about the young, eager county agent going out to tell farmers about the new government programs. He talked to one old farmer sitting in his rocker on the front porch. He told the farmer that the new program would teach farmers how to get more production and have a better life. He, the agent, was there to help.

The old farmer listened and then said, "Son, I ain't farmin' as good as I know how now."

So I am careful with my friends. Do they want their problem solved? I do have to live with them. I'm extra careful, perhaps too careful, when selling my solutions to my friends. The last thing I want is for friends to buy from me because they think my feelings will be hurt if they don't.

But by the same token should we penalize them because they are our friends? If we have a good service or product that we believe in and they need it, shouldn't we offer it? I tell bankers when they are talking to their friends and their friends are happy at another bank to say, "But there is one thing that other bank doesn't have—*me*." People want a friend at the bank. They want a friend in your business. They want a friend in my business. Shouldn't we let them have that friend?

So much of prospecting is making friends, meeting people, listening for problems that we can solve. Donating time to worthy causes can be very gratifying. It is paying back to the community some of what we have gotten. But it can have the side benefit of letting us rub elbows with a different set of people, an opportunity to meet potential clients.

I have several clients who require their key people to spend a certain amount of their time in community service or to belong to a certain number of civic or charitable organizations. Architects, engineering firms, CPAs all have a lot to offer and can gain a lot from these associations. I have seen a few people overdo this approach, by the way. I know one engineer who is so involved in such organizations that he doesn't have time for work or family. Common sense must prevail.

Sandy and Donna Vilas, a couple who teach networking, have written a book called *Power Networking*, published by Duke Publishing of Houston. In case the title frightens you a little, here is a quote that explains their philosophy: "Networking is the genuine expression of interest in others and the willingness to contribute and support when possible."

In the book the Vilas's suggest you have a clear, concise, relatable, and engaging answer to the question, "What do you do?" "You want to be prepared to respond with something other than, 'I am a CPA' or 'I am an attorney.' These responses indicate who you are, not what you do. The important thing to tell people is: what you do, what service you offer, what's special about who you are, and what you do." A first impression can be lasting.

Obviously, this is not all the book says. I recommend it for anyone who is trying to gain more business through contacts.

I have already told you about my client who carries copies of his newsletter in his pocket. This is a great way to develop a mailing list and to connect with people who have problems we can solve. In lieu of a newsletter, company brochures, speeches by the president, and newspaper articles about the company are also effective.

As a trainer I get asked to make speeches to civic clubs and charitable groups. If I'm speaking to a group of business people I offer to send them a copy of "Developing a Marketing Plan for a Small Business," a pamphlet I have written. I ask that they give me their business card with the words "marketing plan" written on it. This gives me a list of those who feel they have a problem with marketing, my prospects.

I have a CPA client who gives talks on small-business taxes. He has put together a pamphlet on the pitfalls of small-business tax planning that he offers in the same manner. Your offering should match your business. Follow-up in a timely manner is essential to make this effective. After sending the information a phone call can determine if any additional interest is in order. The call should be no more than two weeks after the material is sent so it is still fresh in their minds.

Probably the greatest source of prospecting is in a sales call itself. Even is we don't make a sale we often make a friend. This new friend may want to help us find other prospects. A man I know is in the business of providing beepers to business people and individuals of all types. He gets a few dollars a month from thousands of people. It's a good business.

But he tells his salespeople that their call on a prospect is all about getting more prospects. He knows when a prospect agrees to see one of his salespeople that the sales ratio is about one out of two. So his measurement of the effectiveness of a sales call is how many prospects did the salesperson get.

If you truly listen to people's problems and provide workable solutions, they may well want to help their friends who have similar problems. It never hurts to ask.

But just in case you *are* the company, a one-person show, and you need some ideas for expanding your prospecting, here are some. Let's start at the beginning, the chamber of commerce. Every town has one, unless your town is so small that you've known every prospect since he or she was born.

Every chamber has its own membership roster. These are usually available for a small fee or free if you are a member, which you should be if you are in business in that town. In smaller communities the membership roster of a chamber of commerce makes a good starting point for prospects. These are the more forward-thinking businesspeople. They are willing to spend money for progress and to improve their working environment. They tend to be a little more open to change, and change is buying. It is a good start.

Chambers in larger cities not only sell their membership lists but usually have a whole library of directories and even mailing lists. These are usually available for use on the premises or can be purchased or borrowed for a small fee.

Large cities will usually have a firm that builds business mailing lists. The Harris County Business Bureau in Houston stays up to date on all courthouse licenses, permits, etc. It updates these lists periodically. They are available at so much a name with a minimum of a few hundred dollars' worth. HCBB makes these lists available on floppy disks to match your computer. These can be imported directly into software programs such as ACT!

Then there are the direct-mail houses. There is usually at least one in every city of any size. If you are in a small town all of the direct-mail houses have access to nationwide lists that include your community. These lists have gotten very complex, with the ability to give you mailings to certain neighborhoods with demographics that match your product or service. They are organized for business mailings as well. For instance, a swimming-pool-maintenance firm was able to get a list of only those people who have pools in any county in the state.

If you are in a retail business these mailing lists have become very sophisticated. You can target postal carrier routes that are aligned with census tracts that give you such information as income levels and even age categories.

Most of the mail houses will do an entire mailing for you from idea and design to delivery and follow-up.

There are also companies in most cities that will do telemarketing for you. These outfits will even set appointments for your salespeople either charging by the hour or by the appointment. A firm that I work with in the bank consulting business is now using one of these telemarketers to find prospects. They target banks that are in the process of hiring consultants to make the changes we design. Once we have a list of the prospects, setting appointments is easy.

Dun & Bradstreet offers lists with more detailed information about companies. They also offer research information on a membership basis. It is rather expensive but when compared to the cost of your making a poor call the cost is in line.

If you have been in business for any length of time you have a history of gaining successful clients. Use this history to formulate a prospect profile for your company. The first thing I do when writing a marketing plan for a company is to look closely at the company's key clients or customers. By filling out the following form on your customer base you will begin to see patterns develop. The patterns will not only show you what your typical prospect looks like but will give you an idea of what has worked for you in the past in your marketing efforts.

In this form you put the client name in the left column, the year you did the work next, the type of work, and the fee. The "source" shows how you got that client or prospect in the first place. It won't fit all businesses, but with some adaptation it will fit most (see page 163).

What I look for in this form is a pattern of where the business came from, the source. I did this for my business recently and found that over a three-year period some 40 percent of my business came from past customers and old business friends. So from that I focused a larger part of my marketing effort this year on staying in touch with old acquaintances. It has been very effective.

One of the basic tenets of marketing is to look to the past to see from where your growth has come. Barring some major change in your business or industry most of your new growth will come from the same sources.

An addition to the list would be a description of the clients, by

Marketing Planning Background Search

Client Name	Year	Type of work	Dollars	Source

size, income, type of business, etc. Once I built a profile of commercial loan customers for a bank. We looked at their type of business, average loan level, average deposit level, gross sales, income, and net worth. We found that in this particular bank the profile was very narrow. We could define their typical customer in a very neat pattern.

I then took this profile and went to the Dun & Bradstreet file and called up prospects in similar industries with similar profiles in terms of net worth, gross sales, and income. I then called a number of them to see what their banking patterns were. I was amazed, in this case, to find that nine out of ten of these companies had changed banks or tried to change banks in the past two years. We had a ready-made market.

Although you may not have as good financial information on a company as a bank, you probably can make some intelligent guesses. You might find that there are other criteria that define your customer base better. It is a beginning. The more you know about your customer base the better job of prospecting you can do.

One other aspect to consider in prospecting is the idea of incentives for referrals. If you have a number of service people that come in contact with your present customers but are not in the sales end, give them incentives for referring business to your sales staff. The chances are good that your present customers are a good source of new business. You may have ten services in your business and your typical customer may only use one or two. Your service people are in a perfect position to hear comments from your customers that would indicate they have a need for another of your services. An incentive or bonus system will sharpen their listening skills.

A referral is worth ten times as much as a mailing list name. I've already mentioned that I work my referrals first. Whether the referral came from a client, one of your employees, a member of your board, or a friend, the call needs to be made quickly. The referrer needs to get a response and to know that you have followed up.

So now you've found your prospect. Should you call?

Not yet. First there is research. In general, the more you know about a prospect before you call the better off you will be in the call. John Wooden, the great college coach who took the UCLA Bruins to ten National Titles, once said, "Failure to prepare is preparing to fail."

We think of research as poring over a stack of reference material. And it can be just that. But research is gathering information. It doesn't have to be from reference material. It can be from word of mouth. Or it might even be from the prospect.

First, the references. If you are calling on a public company, one listed with the Securities and Exchange Commission, there is a lot of information available to you. Standard and Poor has an annual listing of the past three years' annual reports for all public companies. It gives detailed financial information as well as the company officers by name, the home office and branch locations, some history of the company's business activities, and any problems they have experienced.

Companies registered with the Securities and Exchange Commission also must produce an annual report and a form 10K both of which give detailed information about the company's finances. Often the annual report will also give good information about the company's operation, its successes, its interests. Most companies will send you a copy of these just for asking.

Proxy statements for annual meetings give a lot of information, particularly about the individual officers, directors, and major owners. Only stockholders receive these statements. If the prospect or client is important enough you may want to buy a few shares of their stock.

Also, most public companies have a news release list. You can ask to be put on that mailing list. There is usually a stockholder-relations department to call.

Other reference guides include:

Moody's Manual of Investments
The Thomas Register
City Directories
Industry/Trade Association Publications

If the company is not publicly traded, you will have a more difficult time. For financial information and some history, Dun & Bradstreet, mentioned earlier, is a good source. If many of your clients are in the same industry you might want to belong to their trade organization as a service member. At least get a subscription to that industry's publications.

Sometimes the prospect is the best source of information. Call and ask for company brochures or information about products and services. Drive by the prospect's place of business the night before you are to make a call. What do the premises look like? That can tell you a lot about a company or an individual.

Check your own records. Has this prospect been a customer in the past? If so why did they leave? It helps to be prepared if someone is mad at you. Also, if they have been a customer you may have credit or other pertinent information in your own files.

What is the call history on the prospect? If others have called before, when was it and what happened? If several people from your company are making calls it helps to have a discussion of which calls who will make in the next time period. Someone may say, "I called on that company just last week and there is no sale," or "I read where that company filed Chapter 11, better leave them alone."

Which brings up the final point about research. Research is gathering information. You may get your best information from a member of your staff, a neighbor of the prospect, a business acquaintance, or a competitor of the prospect. In the banking industry I would often call a customer and say, "I'm trying to get your good competitor to come bank with us. What can you tell me about him that I need to know?" You have to be careful with this and know your customer well. But competitors often know a lot about each other.

So to the two questions we give these answers: Q. Where are the prospects? A. Everywhere. Q. How much is enough research? A. As much as you can get.

A final word about research. I'm the world's worst at doing research. At the bank I would jump up from my desk just in time to make the appointment and ask my secretary what we knew about these people as I was putting on my coat. It worked, most of the time. Every now and then I would get egg on my face. Usually, an honest admission of guilt would get me through.

The point of this is, some people who don't like to make sales calls will use research as an excuse not to call. "I don't have enough research. I'm waiting for their annual report." Go ahead. Make the call. The person on whom you are calling probably makes calls, too, and hates to do research. He'll understand.

14

How Did We Get to the End of This Book?

THE steps in a call are these:

1. Preparation:
    - Deciding who to call on, prospecting
    - Research
    - Making the appointment
    - Setting a goal
2. Introduction and rapport development
3. Problem development
4. Summary Feedback
5. Presentation
6. Getting the business
7. Follow-up

We have looked at each of these in the order of their importance. It is time to review these seven steps. There could be six or eight, but I find these to be effective ways to help organize my thinking when I make a call.

Obviously, you can't organize the prospect's reactions or many of the circumstances, so these steps may take one or two or many calls. To complete the development of a client relationship you need them all. To some extent you go through each of them on every call:

1. Preparation

This can't be overstressed. You are a professional—an engineer, architect, banker, etc. You wouldn't think of tackling any of your other tasks without some preparation. If you were an architect you wouldn't think of designing a house, for instance, without many hours of research, conversations with the owner, checks on the lot, the subdivision, and so on. It doesn't make sense, does it?

Under this major heading we have put several subheadings. The first of those is deciding who to call on, prospecting. Prospects are where you find them. They come from everywhere. There are a lot of ideas about where to find them in Chapter Thirteen. Suffice it to say that prospecting is everybody's job—everybody, that is, who wants the company to succeed.

But how do you select the one prospect to call on now? Here are a couple of guidelines.

Get to the easy ones first. There is something in a lot of us that says we have to tackle the hard work or the least desirable work first. I don't think that applies to the business of selling. Success breeds success. If you have a prospect that you think will be an easy sell, see that one first. It will boost your confidence. Besides, it is a much more efficient use of your time.

Another guideline is to always call quickly on any prospects that have been referred to you. These referrals may come from a fellow employee. They may come from a member of your board (get those real quick). They may come from a present customer or even a prospect or maybe just a friend. Any of these sources need to know that you are excited about their referral and that you will act quickly on it. This not only encourages more referrals but it assures that everyone's memory will be fresh: the prospect's memory, the referrer's memory, and yours. Nothing could be worse than having your prospect calling your referrer and having him say, "I don't remember referring you."

Next is research, gathering information about the prospect and his or her company. Information is where you find it. Ask people in your company. Ask your neighbor. Ask the prospect's neighbor or the prospect's competitor but ask. Also, anybody who is going to call on prospects should at least read the local business pages. If there is a business publication in your city, read that. Belong to the chamber of commerce and be involved. Bits of information come along all the time. You never know when you might need it. Curiosity and a sense of wonder are helpful in the research phase as well as the calling phase.

Don't overlook your own company files. Has this prospect been a customer before? It is very embarrassing to call on a prospect, go through the Call Purpose Statement, and then have the prospect say, "I know your company. I did business with you until you assigned that jerk to my account." The prospect is angry and you are caught off guard.

By the way, if the prospect is an ex-customer and you get caught in this situation, relax and listen. I once called with a banker on a fellow who responded to our Call Purpose Statement in almost the way I have shown. He said, "I'll tell you what I think of your bank. I had a guy call on me from there and he was the most obnoxious person I have ever known. He told me how big and important your bank was and how I'd be a fool to bank anywhere else. Well I don't like being called a fool."

I assured our prospect that I would feel the same way had I been treated that way. I asked if he knew the man's name. He opened his desk drawer. "I just cleaned this drawer out last week. I had his card right here until then." He had kept the person's card for many years, just so he could remember how much he hated our bank.

I kept asking questions. I wanted to get him to vent all of his feelings about the situation. I knew he wasn't mad at me. The young banker with whom I was calling had only been with the bank a short while. So we listened.

Finally, when he had run out of gas I said, "We have made notes about this and will check into it for you. But I was fascinated by your displays in the showroom out there. Would you mind taking a few minutes to tell us a little about your business?" We were off and running. I learned all about his business. He had some immense banking problems that were not being solved by his present bank. We left with his financial statements and the bank eventually got all of his business. The poor man had been waiting for years just to tell his story to someone that mattered. He could never tell it as well to his neighbors again.

Then we have to ask for an appointment. This can strike fear in the best of us. It is facing that cold unknown. It is asking for rejection. It takes courage. "Step into your fear."

Here is the first use of the Call Purpose Statement. Why do we want to see the prospect? To tell him about our company? Partly. To learn about the prospect's company? Yes. How do we say that?

"Mr. Training Director, we've been in the business of developing and delivering training programs for companies like yours for the past eighteen years. I've never met you and frankly don't know much about XYZ Corporation. I find that if I'm to stay on the cutting edge of training I have to know about companies like yours and what you are being called on to do in the way of training. I'd like to meet you, let you know a little about us, and find out a little more about you. Would you have time to see me next week?"

It is the smaller version of the Call Purpose Statement. We use it again when we get through the introduction phase in the face-to-face interview. But the prospect needs to know why we want to take up his or her time. If I say I want to come tell you about our company so you will buy my service, I will turn you off from the beginning. No one wants to be sold something. My guess is that if you've stayed with me this long you don't want to "sell" something either. You want to explore goals and problems with me. So say that and you'll probably get lots of appointments.

Then you set a goal. I once had a sales-training instructor that said, "You will increase your sales efficiency by 15 percent just by setting a goal." How did he know? How could you measure such a thing? However, goals do seem to work in my life. My subconscious does seem to be a servomechanism that gets me to my objective. It needs to know what the objective is. So setting a goal for a call can be very effective.

But be careful. Setting too specific a goal prior to the first call can be dangerous. Suppose I decide that my goal is to sell sales training to a prospect whom I haven't met. I go to the office, intent on selling the sales training, and I fail to hear that his real problem is sales management. I miss the clues. The prospect misses the clues. I miss the opportunity for real service and a long-term relationship.

For first calls I sometimes have rather broad goals, like coming back with a genuine problem. That goal is realistic, specific, and measurable, but it does not get in my way of listening for what the problem is. Remember, people buy from us because they have a problem they think we can solve. A goal of establishing the problem may well sharpen my listening and help my focus.

2. Introduction and Rapport Development

You introduce yourself. Then you comment on the things in the office, the office itself, the plaques and pictures on the wall, the appearance of the building, the weather, whatever it takes to get the conversation going.

You have made a note of his or her style. Is he or she a driver, expressive, amiable, or analytical.

If the incumbent is a driver the small talk will probably be short, to the point. It's time for business pretty quickly. You lead in with the Call Purpose Statement. The driver wants to know why you are there and what will take place.

If the incumbent is an expressive there are probably plaques or pictures or trophies that you can ask about. The conversation will take off from there. This is a time to be loose. Listen for jokes. Laugh. Relax and enjoy the show. But look for an opportunity to bring in the Call Purpose Statement. Three or four minutes of small talk is usually enough even for an expressive. But if you continue to open opportunities for conversation it may go for a long time. Then the expressive will get antsy and have to move on. Your interview may be cut short. So listen for the completion of a thought and a pause, though it may be subtle and very brief.

If you are dealing with an amiable, relax and take time to build the relationship. This is a good time to play 'Who do you know?' Take time to assure the amiable that you are interested in him and his concerns, that you like him as a person. You probably will unless you are a driver, in which case now is the time to practice your patience.

The analytical will be a little cool and reserved at first. Analyticals are suspicious of playing "Who do you know?" Plaques on the wall are important to him. If you are a graduate of his college and that plaque is on the wall, by all means comment on it. The plaque wouldn't be there unless the analytical had respect for the institution.

The Transition: The Call Purpose Statement; A Bridge Between Step 2 and Step 3

There is the pause. Pretend the prospect is asking, "Why are you here. What are we going to do?" They probably won't say this, but they are thinking it. Respond.

You have your Call Purpose Statement clearly thought out and carefully rehearsed. If there is a place for memorization, this is it. Have it down so well that you can adjust it to fit the situation, even tie it into the small talk. The knowledge that you can recite this quickly and easily will help you relax. Work on this part.

In the form of review, the Call Purpose Statement should continue to reduce relationship tension while setting the stage for the work to be done, the task tension. It should give the prospect a good reason to talk openly about his or her business, goals, and problems. It should give just enough background about you and your company to give you credibility with the prospect and no more. Then it should show the prospect that talking about their business will help you either in your business or in discussing your business with them.

3. The Problem Development Step

Now the work has started. You are armed with questions, open-ended at first. You listen well and actively. You take notes. You give feedback and make comments, nod your head, say, "I see, tell me about that." You listen for goals and problems. When you hear one you ask more detailed, closed-ended questions.

You and the prospect define the goals and problems together. The prospect may not have clearly understood these goals and problems before you started asking questions. The very process has been helpful to him.

But as you discuss the problems and why they are keeping the prospect from reaching those goals, a motivating factor sets in. The prospect is beginning to feel the pain of the problems, the lack of reaching the goal. Motivation is an inside job. You can help with the questioning/listening process. But the motivation comes from within the prospect's mind.

Since this process may have just now started it may take several more calls before the desire to change is strong enough to buy your solution. So on this call you may give a quick verbal Summary Feedback to show you have listened and understood and then offer to come back later to discuss other ideas and solutions. Or it may be that the process is complete and it is time to present a solution and ask for the business. Either way you follow the steps.

4. The Summary Feedback

As we said in the paragraph above, you may give the Summary Feedback as a verbal response to what you have heard. It usually takes only a few seconds or a minute or two. You hit the highlights. You review a little of the prospect's situation and history. You outline the goals as they have been presented. Then you discuss the problems that are keeping the prospect from reaching those goals.

This verbal recitation of the situation, goals, and problems helps to further clarify them in the minds of the prospect. This may be the first time they have heard them outlined so clearly. There is magic in this process. Not only do you reinforce the motivating factors in the prospect's mind but you show yourself as a concerned outsider who has listened and understood. We all want understanding. Often the process of telling someone else our problems gives us the understanding to move on to a solution. If our solution is the same as the prospects a sale may take place.

But let's say that the ideas we have discussed are still rather new to the prospect. He or she has to do some more thinking about them. They may have to discuss them with others in their organization.

The driver and expressive may want your input to help motivate others with whom they have to work. The analytical may have to let the new ideas simmer in his own mind. He may need to discuss them with others whom he holds in high regard, to get feedback to reinforce his own ideas and opinions, to be sure he is right. The amiable will need to discuss them with others whose relationship gives him reassurance, to know that the team is moving together. Change is difficult and there needs to be time.

Whatever the reason, you sense the timing is not right to ask for change or for the sale, so you decide to offer another visit. You offer to summarize your notes in writing and return later with a written Summary Feedback. You may want to involve someone else in your organization. So you make that suggestion, giving the credentials of the other party who will accompany you on a subsequent visit.

You still get agreement on the next step. That next step in this case may be a time to meet again. Or it may be an agreement to let the prospect think about things and a promise to call next week.

You return to your office and write out a Summary Feedback. You reorganize your notes and present them in terms of background, goals, and problems. The outline logically shows the connection between where the prospect is and where he or she wants to be. You clearly state the problems that are keeping the person from reaching his own goals. This is a formal, written Summary Feedback. It is a powerful instrument.

You share this instrument with others in your organization. You get their input, perhaps rewrite the document. Now you are ready to meet with your prospect again. If you are including another member of your company you prepare enough copies for that person, yourself, the prospect, and any others that may be present in the second meeting.

At that second meeting (or it may be the third, fourth, or more) you present the written document. You, your partner, and the prospect(s) go over it in detail. It brings the prospect back to the first meeting. The goals and problems are clear and in the prospect's conscious thoughts again. It brings any newcomers up to date on the process. It establishes the partnership that you have begun in your first meeting. It moves the motivation process along.

You ask for agreement as to the accuracy of your notes. You make corrections if need be. You now have agreement that you are part of the team that is to seek a solution to the problems outlined. You are ready to ask the question (which you may have asked at the first meeting): "Would you be interested in how we have solved similar problems for some of our other clients?"

If you have gotten this far the answer will undoubtedly be yes. You are ready for your presentation. You have earned the right to suggest change. You are now a partner in seeking a solution. It is a powerful position. It is one of trust. You have developed that level of trust that we agreed early in this book is so important to the loyal customer relationship. You have a willing audience to the next step.

5. The Solution Presentation

This is your moment. This is what you have trained for. You are about to show a prospect how you can solve his problem and help him reach his goals. All of your experience in business is for this event.

You make your presentation. It may be verbal. It may be written. You may use flip charts, graphics, a blackboard, slides, overheads, or those newfangled computer devices. It may be made to one individual. It may be made to a committee or a board. You may play it solo or you may have a staff to assist you. But always keep in mind that it is no more or less than a partner helping to solve the problem as outlined. Answer the questions on the prospect's mind: "What's in it for me? How will this help me reach my goals? Where is the value that will justify the cost?"

You ask for agreement. Does it make sense to the prospect? Will it work in his mind? If not, you make adjustments. You listen to his reasons that he thinks it won't work. You do not get defensive. He is rejecting change, not you. If you have gotten this far with the prospect, he likes you personally. It is change or cost that concerns him.

You repeat his objection in your own words. It is a small version of the problem development step. You give him feedback and show understanding. You reword your solution to meet the newly expressed fears or needs. You ask for agreement again. You flesh out other problems if necessary. Finally, you get agreement.

6. Getting the Business

Now is the moment of truth. You say something like, "Do you think we've gotten a good understanding of your situation, goals, and problems?" You wait for agreement. You've already gotten agreement to all the pieces. You should get agreement to this question.

"Do you like the way we've solved these same problems for our other clients?"

"Yes. It looks good."

"Then, what do you think our next step should be?"

The ball is in the prospect's court.

What you do with what is said is up to you. Is there an objection? Then you treat it as such. You repeat it. You give answers if there are any or you suggest a time to think about it and to come back. It may be an objection you agree with, in which case you close the conversation and see if there are ways you can help.

The answer may be, "I need time to think about it." In my opinion, at this point, you give the prospect time to think about it. You ask how much time it will take and make arrangements to get back in touch then.

It may well be that the answer is, "When do we start?" Or "What does your calendar look like for such and such a date?" In which case you may well be on your way to setting up a new relationship and a new client.

Or you may be a more forward type and instead of the question, "What's our next step?" you ask, "What will it take for us to get your business?" The answers may still be the same. At any rate, you are on your way to a sale or at least a conclusion.

7. Follow-up

Now comes the follow-up. You go back to your office and do the next step, whatever that may be. If you have made a sale then you put the gears in motion to effect the changes necessary to provide the service or product. You notify others in your organization.

You write a letter. You tell the new client what you have done and what he should expect in terms of getting the service or product you have promised. You introduce others in your organization who will be providing the product or service. You set up a lunch with all of the players.

You do the record keeping on both the call and the sale. The calling record on the new client becomes part of that client's permanent file. These notes may come in handy as you sell additional services or as you set up the initial contact.

Calling on Current Clients

Have you learned all of this just to make calls on new prospects? I think not. Everything in this book also applies to your calls on current clients and customers. The process is the same. Only the details change. Here's how.

The preparation step is similar. You have to decide which client to call on but the source is your own company file. You have to do research. But, again, your company files probably hold all the information you need.

Making the appointment should be easy enough. The setting of a goal could be much more specific. You may want to see if this client is a prospect for a new service your company has introduced.

The introduction and rapport development is still an important step. You have a lot of history with which to develop rapport. But remember that there will still be relationship tension. Something new has been added. Your client may never have had a call from your company before. He may think he has done something wrong. I know when one of my bank clients starts calling its customers for the first time about half of them respond with, "Is something wrong? Am I overdrawn?" Relationship tension is always present at the start of a call. If the relationship is strong and of long-standing it may be slight but it will be present. Rapport development is still a necessary endeavor.

The Call Purpose Statement is similar. However, since this is a client that you know and your purpose is, at least partly, to cement good relations, the Call Purpose Statement will be somewhat different than with a prospect. It might go something like this: "Marilyn, you've been a good customer of ours for many years. I think I've been handling your account for nearly three of those years. We really appreciate your business and look forward to many more years of a good relationship. But our company has started a new policy. We feel that if we are going to grow the way we want we are going to have to stay in closer touch with our clients. In order to continue to meet your needs we think we need to come see you, tour your plant, keep up with your changes, and get to know what you're trying to accomplish.

"So the purpose of my call today is to review our relationship, make sure that we are serving you well, and then take some time to get better acquainted with you and your business. You know, I don't think I've ever talked to you about how you got in this business. Would you mind giving me a quick history? I think that would help me handle your account better."

Perhaps you know the client well. Maybe you want to review your files with the client and ask about some specifics that might apply to your new service. In that case your Call Purpose Statement might be, "You and I have been talking about your need to expand. The last time you were in you mentioned that if you got the new contract with XYZ Corporation you would definitely need more room. How is that going? I find it really helps me serve our clients better the more I know about what might be about to happen."

The Call Purpose is still nonthreatening. You are not here to sell something until you find out if there is a problem. And it sets the client up for the task you want to accomplish.

The problem development step is basically the same. The main difference is that you already have a common base of information on which to build. As you use this information be sure that it is, indeed, common. Don't assume that what you think you know is correct and don't assume that the client knows you know it. Give feedback and ask for agreement.

Often when working with one of my clients I will ask them how much they know about their customers. "We know everything. We have to," they may say. I then play a little game with them. I see how many questions I have to ask them before I find something about the customer, even the really good ones, that they don't know. It makes the point.

If you do uncover a problem that you think you can solve with additional or new services or products, the Summary Feedback is the same. You may even want to put it in writing. You may already do this for clients who are taking on new services. It is just as effective and serves all the same good purposes as it does for a new prospect.

The presentation is the same, too. Don't shirk on the planning just because you know this client. He or she deserves the same amount of effort, perhaps more, than you give to a prospect.

The follow-up, too, is basically the same. A brief letter thanking the client for his time and outlining a little of what you have learned is impressive. If a sale has occurred you want to set it up in much the same manner as you would with a new client. Don't penalize your clients for their loyalty.

OK. You've got it all together. You know how it's done. Let's take a look at a case study of a real sales call.

15

It Isn't a Business But We Sold It Anyway

HERE'S a case study. If you want to make a practice exercise out of this case, pretend that you are making a joint call with the banker. See yourself in the prospect's office. Make notes, or use a highlighter to mark what you think are important facts that are brought out in the conversation. Then if you really want to practice, write a Summary Feedback from your highlighted notes before you look at mine.

I use the banker example partly because that is a big part of my background. However, a banker's selling is so well-related to the total company that it offers a fairly universal approach to selling. The banker needs to know about the total company. I hope that if you are not a banker you can translate this sales call to your type of business.

Background

Star Distributing (a fictional name) is in the business of supplying pipes and fittings to the petrochemical industry. It is a Houston company, privately held. I may not have done enough research on the project but I wasn't able to find out much about the company.

I have an appointment with the president, Steve Morrison. I arrive a few minutes early. Mr. Morrison is out on a sales call and has called in to say he will be a few minutes late. I talk to the secretary, ask her a little about the business. Finally she offers to show me the warehouse. After the tour she ushers me into Mr. Morrison's office and brings me a cup of coffee.

179

The desk is cluttered. There are pictures of Morrison and plaques and awards on the wall. I think I have an expressive on my hands but I will hold judgment. Morrison comes in.

Steve: "Hi Dick, I'm Steve Morrison. I'm sorry I'm late. I think I just sold a major account though. Hope you didn't mind the little wait." Big smile, firm handshake.

Dick: "No problem. I had time to visit with your secretary. She really knows your business. She took me through the warehouse."

Steve: "Yes. She's my right hand. She's been with me a long time, really helped me build the business."

Dick: "She tells me you and your wife just got back from San Diego. Vacation, I hope?"

Steve: "Yes. My son is in the Navy and is stationed there. And my sister and her husband live there. So it was mostly family stuff."

Dick: "San Diego is a beautiful city, lots to see and do. My brother lives there. Did you get to do any sight-seeing?"

Steve: "Oh, we always get to the zoo when we're out there. It's a wonderful zoo."

Dick: "Maybe the finest in the country. My brother and his wife always take us there."

There is a pause, Steve shifts in his chair.

Dick: "Well, Steve, the reason I asked to see you—I told you on the phone that I'm with State National Bank. We have really been growing lately. We're particularly interested in expanding the commercial side of our business. We find that if we are going to meet the needs of the commercial community in this part of town we have to get out and get to know the businesses in our area. The more we know about businesses like yours the better job we can do of providing the finest banking available. Now eventually I may want to talk to you about doing some business with us. But right now, my main purpose is to get to know a little about you, your business, what you are doing here. That would really help me and my bank. Would you mind just telling me something about Star Distributing?"

Steve: "Sure. That sounds reasonable. Well, I started Star
Distributing about twelve years ago. I had worked for a
major steel mill in New Orleans."

Dick: Reaching for his briefcase, "Do you mind if I take notes?"

Steve: "No. That's fine. We're talking about my favorite subject,
you know. Sure, take all the notes you want.

"I was in sales, basically the same stuff I'm selling
now. I grew up in Houston and when I decided to branch
out on my own I started here. And I also came to Houston
because—well, for one thing, I had a geographical
noncompete clause—but this is about the best market for
my products."

Dick: "What are your products. What do you sell?"

Steve: "Well, we are sort of a combination manufacturers' rep
and distributor. Our strength seems to be selling
specialized steel pipe. You know, we serve the oil patch as
well as the petrochemical industry. We have several lines
of specialized stainless steel pipe that is in very high
demand these days. We've been able to get some very
good lines."

Dick: "When your secretary took me through the warehouse I
saw that you had a good many small fittings and so on.
Who particularly are your customers? Who do you sell
these to?"

Steve: "Well, some of the major engineering and construction
firms like Fulor and Lumus and David International and
a lot of the smaller firms, too."

Dick: "So, you become a subcontractor then, when they're
putting together specialized plans?"

Steve: "Yeah. Well, the way it works is that they design these
massive installations. They will go in and design a whole
plant and we try to stay in very close contact with them in
order to make sure that they are specifying materials that
we supply. We have developed a very good relationship
with them over the years. We stress our high reliability
and so on."

Dick: "Uh-huh."

Steve: "And so when that's written into the specifications then
we become the supplier, the prime supplier for their

installations, you know, in this specialized end of the work."

Dick: "Then you actually provide the pipes and fittings and so on to the subcontractor who is installing that part of the plant? Is that right?"

Steve: "Yes."

Dick: "But you are not in the construction business as such, are you?"

Steve: "No. From time to time we have been involved in helping to find a contractor or a subcontractor...for a given specialty...because we are so closely in touch with what's going on in the industry."

Dick: "Uh-huh. And this area you deal with might be a specialized segment of a much larger piece of equipment or installation that they are putting in?

Steve: "Yes. As you know—or I don't know if you are familiar with that business or not—a company like Fulor may or may not be the prime contractor. That is, they may be just the engineering firm that draws up all the plans and specs but another firm may be the prime contractor."

Dick: "In that case you might actually work with them in setting up specifications but then would have to bid separately on the use of your particular fittings or..."

Steve: "That's right."

Dick: "But since you were involved in the actual setting up of the engineering you would certainly have the inside track on the sale of the fittings when that time came. Is that a fair assumption?"

Steve: "Well, yes and no. It's not only a matter of just bid. Obviously these major companies do have purchasing policies that require them to speak to several different people but they take service and our reputation into consideration. So being in close contact with them, I think, is one of the primary things, as well as constantly reinforcing our reputation for good, prompt service."

Dick: "Uh-huh. And of course that becomes a very important part, I would think, of your type of business, since this is a specialized end of it and, I assume, that it's not a major part of that total construction project.

"By the way, you mentioned you have some good lines. Who are your suppliers? Who do you sell for?"

Steve: "Well, we represent a wide variety of firms that manufacture steel pipes and fittings. Some of our lines are quite specialized. Stainless steel, chrome, and some of this very exotic alloyed steel. In fact some of our suppliers have their own sales force and their own warehouses but they can't be everywhere at once so we supplement their efforts in these specialized areas."

Dick: "Oh, is that right? So you would actually buy, say, from Behemouth or some of the larger companies?"

Steve: "Yes, indeed. Behemouth and International Steel as well as other specialized firms that don't have their own sales organization."

Dick: "Uh-huh. The smaller industries. But apparently you do have a number of suppliers or you represent a number of various companies, then."

Steve: "Yeah. We have about thirteen different major suppliers and then quite a few smaller ones."

Dick: "Do you have any problems associated with suppliers?"

Steve: "No, not so much a supply problem. Unless it's some highly specialized item that's not a production item...but most of the production items...there's ample supply at the moment. As you probably know, most of the major steel companies have been refitting to better compete with the Japanese. So between them our items are readily available.

"But since you mention problems, it's not a supply problem from the manufacturer, it's our growth."

Dick: "What do you mean?"

Steve: "Well, our business has been growing. As we grow we have to have more inventory. That costs money. We have to carry more accounts receivable. That costs money. I guess if we have a problem it's finding the money to keep up with the growth."

Dick: "Yes. I noticed in my tour of your warehouse that it looked kind of crowded."

Steve: "Yeah. We're on top of each other here."

Dick: "Based on my knowledge of the industry I would guess

that there's a lot of money tied up in inventory. That type of material is pretty expensive, is it not?"

Steve: "Yes. It really is. Well, we'll probably do about ten million in sales this year. We have about five or six turns a year so my guess is we've got about two million back in that warehouse. It doesn't look like it, does it?"

Dick: "Pretty high-priced stuff."

Steve: "Yes it is."

Dick: "So that's pinching your cash flow pretty badly?"

Steve: "Yeah. We're handling it but I've had to extend my payment time. I don't like to be late on payables but it seems to be part of the industry standard."

Dick: "With the kind of growth you're talking about this could get to be a serious problem, could it not?"

Steve: "Well, yes and no. I guess the biggest problem is that I've gone about as far as I can go growth wise. That bothers me a little. Although I'm not sure I want to get much bigger. I just can't say. I stay pretty busy as it is."

Dick: "So your growth is limited?"

Steve: "Yes, pretty much. As I get more business there is more out in receivables, more in payables, and more in inventory. I didn't know when I started this business that success would be so expensive. My wife says, 'If you're making so much money, where is it?' It's back there in the back, that's where is is."

Dick: "Well, I don't want to downplay your problems but these are the problems I see in many young, aggressive, fast-growing companies. This is a classic example of growing pains."

Steve: "Yeah. I guess these are good kinds of problems to have. I'd hate to have the opposite."

Dick: "Quite true. Tell me about your sales force. With this kind of growth they must be pretty good."

Steve: "Well, we've got seven employees. There are five salespeople, counting myself, and the inside sales guy. The other two are my secretary and a handyman-type, does deliveries, maintenance, whatever."

Dick: "You mentioned five salesman counting yourself. Do you spend a good bit of your time outside selling?

Steve: "Not as much as I would like to. I get tied in here more
        than I would really choose to if I could do something
        about it. But I like the selling. That's how I got started.
        That's the part of the business that turns me on.
        Managing all this money is not very exciting to me."

Dick: "Really? Tell me something about your background."

Steve: "Well, I was a salesman for Behemouth Steel for ten years
        and then I worked for another manufacturer's rep in New
        Orleans for five years. I've been selling these same types
        of products the whole time. I worked here in Houston part
        of the time I was with Behemouth. I'm from here. That's
        why I started the business here."

Dick: "And I guess Houston is a good market for your products,
        maybe as good or better than New Orleans."

Steve: "You bet, one of the best markets in the country. But we
        have sort of sneaked back over to the New Orleans area. I
        now have a man who covers the Mississippi River area.
        My noncompete clause ran out a long time ago."

Dick: "So you do get over as far as New Orleans?"

Steve: "You bet. We cover a good part of south Louisiana and go
        as far west as Corpus Christi. Probably 60 percent of our
        sales are here in the greater Houston area, but that other
        40 percent is a pretty important. And the Mississippi area
        is growing. There's a good bit of construction along the
        river. Someday I may want to put a branch in Lake
        Charles."

Dick: "Oh, is that right?"

Steve: "Yeah, or Lafayette or one of those towns."

Dick: "Are all of your salespeople located in Houston now?"

Steve: "Yes. They all travel out of Houston now and so they will
        go out there on a route, a pretty regular route. You know,
        you don't have that many different customers so it's pretty
        easy to manage from a central location. I find that it just
        makes communication a lot easier. Well, let me change
        that a little. There are advantages both ways. If I had a
        branch in south Louisiana and maybe one in Victoria or
        closer to Corpus, it might help our communications with
        the clients. So I may want a couple of branches...if I can
        solve the growth puzzle, that is."

Dick: "The need for expanded working capital, you mean?"

Steve: "Right."

Dick: "If you could solve the financial problems, would you expand by adding branches?"

Steve: "Probably not at first. What I need to do is add people here in Houston first. As we expand our sales in those other areas then we would probably move some of those people to the branch... you know, just a small office.

"But a chicken or egg kind of thing. I don't want to open a branch without having the business to support it. I can't get the business to support it without the people and we're out of space here.

"I guess all the problems are kind of interrelated. I can't grow without people. I can't add people without adding space. I can't add space, people, or inventory without more money, and more money comes from more sales. It's kind of a vicious cycle isn't it." He was almost talking to himself at this point. His eyes were looking at the ceiling.

Dick: "These are the kinds of problems we deal with all the time, Steve. By the way, do you have plans to expand or rent a larger space?"

Steve: "Well, I've been looking. Our lease is up here in another year. I've got a five-year option but I have sort of had in the back of my head that I would like to own my own building."

Dick: "Have you done anything along the line of buying property? Have you looked?"

Steve: "Not really. I should have been. Oh I've looked at a couple of spots. I don't know. You get so bogged down in the day-to-day operations that you don't have time to do the long-range stuff. Come to think of it, that lease is up in less than a year. Maybe you've spurred me a little. I need to get on that."

Dick: "This is another typical problem we find with businesses the size of yours. You're not large enough to have a full-time person to manage the finances and long-range planning, yet there is some definite work that needs to be done in that area."

Steve: "I've got a good CPA. She keeps pushing me in this
direction, says I need more planning and I need to be
looking out for the cash flow problem. But she's busy with
other clients. But you're right. I'm feeling the need for
that now."

Dick: "Well as I look over my notes it seems that most of your
concerns tie back to the overriding problem of cash flow.
However, judging by what you've said about growth, your
business must have been pretty profitable to provide the
cash flow it has."

Steve: "Yeah, the gross profit is pretty good. My operating
expenses are pretty high though. If I do the ten-million
gross this year I'll probably put a little less than a million
on the bottom line...that includes my salary. But I pay
pretty good bonuses. When I went in business I decided I
wanted to build a company with good long-term people. In
order to do that you have to pay them. I also have a good
profit-sharing program. As a result we have very little
employee turnover. These folks have been with me for
some time now."

Dick: "Uh-huh. And I would think that ties directly back in with
what you said earlier about having a reputation for good
service and so you get repeat business."

Steve: "You bet."

Dick: "If you reach your ten-million this year, where would you
set your goal for the following year?"

Steve: "I was talking to my head salesperson about that the other
day. I think it's reasonable to sustain a 20 percent growth,
say to twelve million for the following year. That is, if I
can find the finances to support it." His voice dropped a
little.

Dick: "Yeah. That continues to be a problem, doesn't it? You
mentioned profit-sharing. Who manages that fund for
you?"

Steve: "Right now I've got it in CDs. We've got about half a
million in it, though. I keep thinking I need to get
someone to manage that. Time. You know."

Dick: "Well in the way of review it looks like you have built the
kind of company that you want to live with. It's built on a

good solid reputation. People are in place to maintain that reputation. I'm impressed with what I see. This is the kind of business we like to work with.

"I'm wondering, though, has your bank been out to go over some of these problems with you?"

Steve: "Well, they've been with me from the start."

Dick: "Where do you bank, by the way?"

Steve: "I'm at F&M. They've gotten pretty big but Jim Wilson over there, I've known him for years. I think he would do pretty much what we asked him to do. We've been trying to finance our growth out of profits. I do borrow a little from time to time. You know, the cash flow problem. I don't know. I think I owe him about fifty thousand or so."

Dick: "And this is the only borrowing you do, about fifty thousand?"

Steve: "Yeah. I may have gotten up to a hundred thousand a time or two. I'm pretty conservative. I don't want to get overextended. I've tried to finance my growth with profits. I don't know. I may have gotten to the point where that won't work anymore."

Dick: "Has Jim been out here?"

Steve: "Well, I've been trying to find the time to invite Jim to come out. You know he's really busy. They just made him senior VP for commercial lending. It's pretty tough for him to get out. But he's really a fine guy. Anything I've ever asked him to do, they've found a way to do it."

Dick: "Good. Well, changing the direction a little, where would you say is the greatest area of opportunity for growth in the future? Will you stay with your main line or are there other directions you've considered?"

Steve: "Well it's interesting that you've mentioned that. Most of our products are now sold for new installations, but, you know, we've begun to break into the replacement business by inertia. I mean, we've had some business that comes in over the transom. You know, call-in business."

Dick: "Because people know you since you were there at the installation?"

Steve: "Yeah. I think that could be a very profitable adjunct to the present business. I would really like to expand into that area."

Dick: "Are there any particular problems that getting into that area would give you?"

Steve: "Well it requires a totally different marketing approach and it could call for a major expansion of inventory. Then you're more like a parts house. You have to have what they need when they need it or you don't get any of that business."

Dick: "But it is probably pretty profitable. Right?"

Steve: "Right. It's very profitable because when they need a replacement part, they need it fast. They need it now, because that part of their plant is down and in a continuous-process operation downtime is very expensive. They usually don't quibble overprice. So it requires a completely different marketing approach. I'd have to have the inventory. I'd probably also have to have one person working just on that type of sale, a replacement part expert. That person would go around behind the salespeople I have now and get acquainted. He would have to manage the whole thing. It would take a special type of person. But I would like to look into that."

Dick: "Again, you are looking at cash flow problems. You'd probably be looking at a fairly highly paid person plus the cost of more inventory."

Steve: "Yeah. I would have to get an experienced person. I don't think any of the fellows I have now would really be right for that. You really need to find someone from another company that's doing that now. That means I would have to pay for it."

Dick: "Well all of this is really interesting. I've seen a lot of exciting things about your business. I really think your future is pretty much unlimited. If you don't mind, let me get just a couple of detailed questions out of the way. What I'd like to do is go back to my office, reorganize my notes, and write them up. I find this is a pretty good discipline and it helps in communicating what I've learned about you to some of the other officers at our bank. I'd like them to know about you, too. I might send you a copy so you could see if I have a pretty good feel for your business. So a couple of things we haven't covered. You're a corporation, are you not?"

Steve: "Yes. We incorporated in '84."

Dick: "And you're the sole stockholder?"

Steve: "Yes. I've thought about offering some stock options but I haven't yet. My wife and son are on the board but they are not active in the company."

Dick: "Will your son be coming into the company?"

Steve: "Well I don't know. He's in the Navy now and will have to finish his college degree when he gets out. I don't know if he will be interested in the business or not. I'd like to have him."

Dick: "Well, Steve, it looks like I've got a pretty good picture of your organization. You've put together a pretty good company. It looks like the only problem you don't quite have a solution to is the cash flow problem. We've got a guy at the bank who has gotten to be a pretty good expert in the kind of financing you're looking at. Would you mind my going over my notes with him and maybe seeing if he'd like to come visit with you? He might have some ideas that would be worth your looking at."

Steve: "That sounds great. You've really made me do some thinking about where the company is going."

Dick: "Well, let me get my thoughts down on paper, get with him, and then I'll get back to you."

Steve: "Fine. I'll look forward to hearing from you."

There is the story. Often I have people ask me if people will really open up to you that much. The answer is, yes. I find that if you show a real interest in people they love to talk about their business and what they do for a living. The only thing that is not typical about this call is that it is so short. I often spend over an hour with a prospect like this.

Now the work begins. I have to write a Summary Feedback. You might want to try your hand at it before you see what I have done. Then see how it compares with what I have put together.

SUMMARY OF UNDERSTANDING

The following is a summary of my understanding of your situation, goals, objectives, and areas of concern. Please read it carefully to see if I have a complete understanding. Please let me know of any mistakes, corrections, or additions you would like for me to make.

Background Summary

Star Distributing was incorporated in 1984 and is owned 100 percent by Steve Morrison. The Company is sort of a combination between a manufacturers' rep and a distributor providing specialized pipe and fittings to the oil patch and the petrochemical industry. The following additional information seems pertinent to our study:

- The Company has seven employees. Five, including Steve, are in sales. There is one secretary and a delivery/maintenance person. Most of the employees have been with the Company for a long time. There is little or no employee turnover due at least in part to a good compensation program, annual bonuses, and a profit-sharing program. There is about $500,000 in the profit-sharing plan now. It is all in CDs.
- Star has some thirteen major suppliers and several smaller ones. They distribute specialty items for such major steel mills as Behemouth and International even though these firms have their own sales force and warehouses. Star either handles specialty items or covers geographic territory that their sales force cannot cover.
- In addition, Star handles all sales in this territory for a few small mills that specialize in stainless steel, chrome, and high allow pipes and fittings.
- Star covers a territory roughly from New Orleans to Corpus Christi, primarily along the Texas and Louisiana coasts. However, about 60 percent of the business comes from the greater Houston area. All of the Company's salespeople live and work out of Houston, however. Much of the selling is working with major design/construction companies in incorporating their products into the design.
- The Company has had good growth and profits through the

years. Steve expects the company to do about $10 million in gross sales this year with a profit just under $1 million, including his salary. This profit comes in after bonuses and profit sharing for the staff. Steve likes to pay well in order to keep good people. This ties in to an overall philosophy of keeping an excellent reputation for good and fast service.

- The Company banks with F&M Bank. The loan officer on the account is Jim Wilson. Steve has borrowed as much as $100,000 in the past and owes about $50,000 now.
- Steve has considered setting up stock options for his key salespeople but has not done so at this time. He is the sole stockholder. His wife and son are on the board but not active in the Company.

Objectives

1. To reach $10,000,000 in sales this year with a profit of just under $1,000,000.
2. To expand sales to $12,000,000 next year for a 20 percent increase.
3. To open branches in Louisiana and South Texas.
4. To expand into the after market supplying replacement parts for the same industries that use his first-time installations.
5. To own his own building with room for growth.

Areas of Concern

1. The main area of concern seems to be a pinch on cash flow caused by growth. This problem is restraining growth.
2. Steve expressed concern that he doesn't have enough people or time to manage the finances and do long-range planning.

We showed this to my fellow loan officer back at the bank, and he and I planned our approach for another call the next week. The first thing we did on that call was to let Steve read this over while we followed along. Our proposed solution tied right into the Summary of Understanding. It is a hypothetical case but we hypothetically got the business. Jim Wilson should have used this system on his present good customers.

Thanks for coming along on the call. I hope you can see how this relates to your business, whether you are a banker or not. Applying this example to your own needs should be fairly easy.

16

Trudging the Road

At the end of my selling seminar I ask how many people feel a little more comfortable with making a sales call. Usually a majority of the hands go up. A few tell me they were not uncomfortable to start with. One or two say that are still terrified.

If you have stayed with me this far, I would guess that you were among the ones who had some discomfort with the idea of selling. I hope that you would have held up your hand if I had asked the question of you.

The last thing I ever wanted to be was a salesman. I went to college, in part, so I wouldn't have to sell anything. After my disastrous experience selling books door-to-door I was really convinced that selling was not for me.

So I entered the field of chamber of commerce management after graduating. I thought chamber managers went around being nice to people in the community. Guess what? I found out that a chamber manager's main job is selling. I had become a salesman. It was years before I admitted it to anyone, especially myself.

Perhaps that is the reason I have spent so much of my adult life teaching people that it is all right to sell, that selling is helping to solve problems. Actually, everyone sells something. Kids sell their parents on letting them do what they want. Parents sell their kids on doing what they should. Managers sell employees on doing a good job. Some people have to sell their peers on their idea for a new project. Volunteers in charitable organizations have to sell. Politicians have to sell us to get our vote. As a matter of fact, the few statesmen I can think of are really the best at selling.

To be sure there will always be the salesperson who is in it to find better ways to manipulate others into buying something they don't want. There is always the stigma of the used-car salesman barking his wares. But the truth of the matter is that most used-car salespeople are really hard-working people trying to provide a service to their customers. We just don't buy from the other kind. They eventually get the picture and change their ways or find another line of work.

I said at the beginning that I don't know why you picked up this book to read. I can only assume that you don't want to be a salesperson. But you find for one reason or another that you have to sell. If I have opened your thinking to the fact that just maybe selling could be a marvelous part of the business of life then I have been successful. If not, then I hope I have made you a little more comfortable with the whole process. If selling is part of your life then it should be comfortable. Perhaps someday it can even become enjoyable.

I wish you luck, whatever you do. I'll leave you with a story that might be a value. I know it has meant a lot to me.

It is the story of Raymond Wilkins. That's not his real name but he was a real person and this is a real story. Raymond grew up in a small town in Central Texas, a town not greatly touched by present-day problems. There was one bank in town, a few stores, and about 4,000 people. If you went to this town you were headed there. You didn't accidentally pass through it.

I had gone to the town on a Friday evening to prepare for a bank director's workshop I was holding on the following morning. I went to the bank about closing time. The bank president sent a young vice president to make sure my room was OK. I was staying in the town's only motel. It was adequate.

Then we went to the area's finest restaurant. It was twenty miles away in another little town. That was where I first met Raymond. As we entered the restaurant I heard a ruckus over in the corner. I looked and there were about ten people sitting around a big table. There was laughter and good humor.

There was one man who was leading the party. He was the center of attention, the cut-up, the man with the big warm laugh and the clever phrases. I learned later that it was Raymond Wilkins. He had family visiting from out of state. This was his birthday and he was having a party. Then I noticed that Raymond was not moving much; in fact, not at all. His wife was feeding him birthday cake.

He was in a wheelchair. A large plastic bottle was stuffed in his arm. His only movement was to shift his head just enough to drink water from a straw in the bottle. Raymond had multiple sclerosis, a crippling disease in its later stages. He was paralyzed from the neck down.

As the party broke up, Raymond had his wife wheel him over to my table. "You're Dick Kendall, aren't you?" Up close his smile was infectious.

"Yes, I am."

"I wanted to meet you. I know you're here for our board workshop. I'm really excited about it and what our bank is doing. I think we've got a great bunch of guys. But I can't attend. You see I've got company, and they don't get this far from home very often. I've got to play host."

Then he thought a minute. "If I can get them to go into Houston shopping would you mind my coming in late?" I assured him I wouldn't mind and told him to try and make it.

After Raymond had gone, the bankers began to tell me about him. He had grown up here. He was well liked, came from a good, prosperous family. He had become a county judge when the disease was in its early stages. He now was a city judge—about all the work he could manage.

But they told me he was always about town, visiting, cheering people on, showing concern for the needs of others. He had a helper who pushed his chair around for him. He came by the bank every day, they told me. He always had a word of encouragement for anyone who needed it. The teller line looked forward to his daily visits.

"We take him hunting on the weekends, too," one of the bankers added.

"Hunting?" I said.

"Yeah. He always loved to hunt as a kid." I knew the area was noted for its winter goose hunting. "Now he'll call us up and say, 'Are you goin' hunting?' We say, 'Yes,' and he says, 'Come get me.' So we go by and get him early in the morning. He's got his hunting clothes on. We put him out by us in a lawn chair. We cover him up so the geese can't see him. He laughs and cuts up with us and has more fun than anyone. He loves it."

The next morning I was doing my thing with the directors. We were on a large screened-in porch at a lake house owned by one of the directors. About mid-morning a car pulled up. Raymond's driver took him out of the car and wheeled him onto the porch. The whole mood of the meeting changed. Things were lighter. Raymond's comments were lifting, almost inspiring. It was one of my better workshops.

At lunch I noticed that Raymond looked over to the man next to next to him and asked him to cut up his sandwich and feed him. Apparently everyone was comfortable with this solution to the problem, and this wasn't the first time it had been employed.

After lunch Raymond asked me to sit down and visit with him. I did. He said, "Dick, can I ask you a personal question?"

I said, "Sure."

He said, "When you ended our workshop you looked at each of us and said you saw something special, that you liked what you saw. Now tell me the truth. Do you tell every group that or did you really feel like we have something special?"

I laughed. "Well, Raymond, if I've got a bunch of turkeys I don't tell them that. I don't tell them they're special unless I really feel it. I'm impressed with what I see here. I think you're headed in a good direction." I was impressed. I didn't add that much of my being impressed had to do with him. Perhaps I should have.

Then for some reason this question popped into my head. I don't know why I asked it. If I had thought about it I probably wouldn't have. But I'm so glad I did.

I said, "Raymond, can I ask you a personal question?"

He, too, said, "Sure."

I said, "Raymond, with your obvious handicap, how do you keep such a marvelous attitude about life?" I couldn't believe I had said that. For a second I was so afraid I had offended him. People just don't ask questions like that. But I'm so glad I did. Here is what he said.

"Well, Dick, I don't know." He was not at all offended but I don't think he had ever been presented with the question before. "You know, this thing came on me slowly. First, I fell down a lot, didn't know why. Then I lost the use of my legs. It would always level off for a while after each new phase."

He looked off at the ground, with a thoughtful look on his face.

Then he looked back at me. I felt he was checking to see if he could trust me with the secret.

"I guess to answer your question...Every morning when my wife wheels me over to the basin to shave me I have time to look at myself in the mirror and think about the day. I look at me sitting in my chair, at this body that's not of much use anymore. Then I look me in the eye and I say to myself, 'Raymond, this is what we've got to work with today. Now what are we going to do to make it the finest day it can possibly be?"

That story is in here because it's a story that needs telling. Raymond was an A1 salesman. He sold me on his little town. He sold his fellow board members on doing it better. He sold me and everyone else on Raymond. But most of all he sold Raymond on life.

I don't know what your life is like, what problems you face, even what your business is. But I hope whatever it is you now have some new tools to make it work. And maybe you, like me, will put a little sticky note with the word RAYMOND on your mirror and make every today the best day it can possibly be.

Good luck. I hope we meet somewhere as we trudge the road to happy destiny.

Index